Stars
by Magic

New Super-Easy Technique!

Diamond-Free® Stars from Squares & Rectangles!

Perfect Points and No Y-Seams!

Nancy Johnson-Srebro

C&T PUBLISHING

Text © 2004 Silver Star, Inc.

Artwork © 2004 C&T Publishing

Publisher: Amy Marson

Editorial Director: Gailen Runge

Editor: Liz Aneloski

Technical Editors: Ellen Pahl, Carolyn Aune

Copyeditor/Proofreader: Stacy Chamness

Cover Designer/Design Director/Book Designer: Kristy A. Konitzer

Illustrator: John Heisch

Color Consultant: Sharon Schamber

Production Assistant: Matt Allen

Quilt Photography: Sharon Risedorph, unless otherwise noted

Digital How-To Photography: Diane Pedersen and Luke Mulks

Published by C&T Publishing, Inc., P.O. Box 1456, Lafayette, California, 94549

Front cover: *Morning Star* by Sharon Schamber

Back cover: *Medallion Chorus* by Nancy Johnson-Srebro, quilted by Veronica Nurmi

No-Fail® and Quilt Map® are registered trademarks of Silver Star, Inc. Diamond-Free® is a registered trademark of Silver Star, Inc.

Attention Teachers: C&T Publishing, Inc. encourages you to use this book as a text for teaching. Contact us at 800-284-1114 or www.ctpub.com for more information about the C&T Teachers Program.

We take great care to ensure that the information included in this book is accurate and presented in good faith, but no warranty is provided nor results guaranteed. Having no control over the choices of materials or procedures used, neither the author nor C&T Publishing, Inc. shall have any liability to any person or entity with respect to any loss or damage caused directly or indirectly by the information contained in this book. For your convenience, we post an up-to-date listing of corrections on our web page (www.ctpub.com). If a correction is not already noted, please contact our customer service department at ctinfo@ctpub.com or at P.O. Box 1456, Lafayette, California, 94549.

Trademarked (™) and Registered Trademark (®) names are used throughout this book. Rather than use the symbols with every occurrence of a trademark and registered trademark name, we are using the names only in the editorial fashion and to the benefit of the owner, with no intention of infringement.

Library of Congress Cataloging-in-Publication Data

Johnson-Srebro, Nancy.

 Stars by magic : new super-easy technique! diamond-free® stars from squares & rectangles! perfect points and no y-seams! / Nancy Johnson-Srebro.

   p. cm.

   ISBN 1-57120-241-2 (paper trade)

1. Patchwork--Patterns. 2. Quilting--Patterns. 3. Patchwork quilts. 4. Stars in art. I. Title.

 TT835.J5868 2004

 746.46'041--dc22

Printed in China

10 9 8 7 6 5 4 3 2 1

IMPORTANT LEGAL NOTICE:

The methods and techniques shown in this book for making Eight-Point Star designs are Patent Pending and protected by U.S. and International Copyright laws against unauthorized use and infringement. Eight-Point Star designs that are made from rectangle and square geometric shapes, or combinations thereof, are also protected. Readers of this book are permitted to make Eight-Point Star designs using the patterns in this book for personal use only. Any duplication or commercial use of these methods, techniques, and designs is strictly prohibited without written authorization in advance by the author.

Dedication

This book is dedicated to you, the quilters of the world. I hope it brings you some small measure of the pleasure I have had in writing it. Without your encouragement to grow as a person, quilter, and author, this book would not have been possible. I thank you very much.

Acknowledgments

I offer special thanks to my biggest fans . . . my husband, children, and granddaughter, Casey. You all mean the world to me.

I give a wholehearted thank you to my quilt team:

Karen Bolesta, Karen Brown, Debbie Donowski, Janet McCarroll, Ellen Pahl, Marcia Rickansrud; and master quilters, Veronica Nurmi and Sharon Schamber. You unselfishly gave of your time, talent, and knowledge. Your friendship keeps me going in good times and bad.

Special thanks to Jeannette Kitlan, owner of my local quilt shop, Endless Mountains Quiltworks.

Also to the entire C&T Staff, Publisher Amy Marson, my editor, Liz Aneloski, and Darra Williamson. Thank you for recognizing how important this Diamond-Free method is, and for shifting priorities to get the word out as quickly as possible.

Lastly but certainly not least, I offer a sincere thank you to the following companies whose products were used in this book.

American & Efird

Bernina® of America

Clearwater Fabrics

Clothworks

Fairfield Processing Corporation

FreeSpirit

Just Another Button Company

K1C2 Solutions/EK Success

Mountain Mist

P&B Textiles

Prym Dritz Corporation/Omnigrid®

Quilting Creations International

Red Rooster Fabrics

RJR Fashion Fabrics

Robert Kaufman Co., Inc.

Starr Designs

Superior Threads

The Warm Company

Timeless Treasures

PAGE 18

PAGE 34   PAGE 36

PAGE 20   PAGE 22

PAGE 48

PAGE 24

PAGE 38   PAGE 50

PAGE 26   PAGE 28   PAGE 40   PAGE 42

PAGE 30   PAGE 32   PAGE 44   PAGE 46

PAGE 58   PAGE 61   PAGE 64   PAGE 66   PAGE 68

PAGE 71   PAGE 74   PAGE 76   PAGE 78   PAGE 80

PAGE 52   PAGE 54

PAGE 56

Contents

Introduction	6
Quilting Basics	7
Diamond-Free® Method	11
How to Read the Charts	17
Blocks 1–30	18
Using Directional Fabrics	82
Bonus Blocks and Borders	84
Thinking Inside the Block	86
Quilt Maps 1–10	88
Resources	127
About the Author	128

INTRODUCTION

Quilts have changed a great deal since I first got hooked on quiltmaking as a starry-eyed girl many years ago. Then, most of the quilts showed the influence of the simple days of the past, using traditional geometric shapes. Occasionally, I would see a more elaborate pattern showing the quilter's creativity and skills. But using simple blocks was the norm. I've seen quiltmaking rise to new heights since my childhood, with a great movement toward more complex designs and embellishments with threads, beads, and so on. I appreciate these new art forms and have dabbled in them myself. However, I still prefer simple yet elegant patterns, accurately pieced and quilted to perfection.

One of my very favorite blocks is the traditional Eight-Pointed Star. For years in my classes I had seen quilters shy away from making this block. I had also experienced the problems of cutting 45° diamonds and working with bias edges and set-in seams.

I knew there had to be an easier way to make these beautiful stars without the hassle! I experimented and cut untold yards of fabric trying to piece the Eight-Pointed Star design in different ways. My labor of love started many years ago, but I really got into it while writing *Block Magic* and *Block Magic, Too!* Then, after two years of heavy experimenting with squares and rectangles, I finally found the magic to Eight-Pointed Stars and developed my "Diamond-Free" method. Was all this work worth it? I think so, and I think you will too after using the technique. Accurate Eight-Pointed Star blocks—without dealing with diamond shapes, bias edges, and set-in seams—await you!

You don't have to stop at just making Eight-Pointed Stars. I've used this innovative method to sew Lone Stars, Baskets of Flowers, and many original star blocks. And don't be concerned with the cutoffs from this method; you can use these pieces to create original bonus wall-hangings and quilts that complement the original Eight-Pointed Star project! The design and décor possibilities are endless.

Of course, no book of mine would be complete without some user-friendly Quilt Maps to help you design a complete quilt. So, I invite you to go ahead and start cutting squares and rectangles. The sky really *is* the limit. The starry-eyed girl is still around, and here's proof!

Quilting BASICS

ROTARY CUTTING EQUIPMENT

The quality of the rotary cutting equipment you use for quiltmaking makes all the difference in how good the finished quilt will look. Use accurately printed rulers, such as Omnigrid products, along with a good-quality cutting mat. Also, be sure to use a rotary cutter that is suited for your personal style and physical needs. I've found that either the Dritz 45mm or Omnigrid 45mm pressure-sensitive rotary cutter allows me to rotary cut for hours without hand fatigue.

Omnigrid rulers have always been my favorite, and now I've worked with Omnigrid to make my favorite rulers even better! We've designed a new ruler called the Diamond-Free Omnigrip ruler. This user-friendly 6" x 14" ruler is designed for quilters who mainly cut strips, squares, and rectangles, hence the 30°, 45°, and 60° angle markings have been eliminated.

The highlighted 1/4" areas around the edge of the ruler make precise trimming of the 1/4" seam allowance quick and easy—perfect for my Diamond-Free star method!

MY FAVORITE THINGS

I prefer the Omnigrid mat because it's reversible—green on one side and light gray on the other side. I use the light gray side for cutting because fabrics show up well.

NO-FAIL ROTARY CUTTING

Believe it or not, there are only two shapes used throughout the star block patterns in this book—a square and a rectangle. Both are very easy to rotary cut. The photos that follow show the cutting technique for a left-handed or a right-handed person.

Cutting a Square

1. The cutting chart for each block gives the cut measurement of a square. This will determine the width of the strip you will cut. For example, if the instructions require four 3" x 3" squares, cut a 3" x 13" strip of fabric. Always cut the strip a little longer than necessary; this will allow you to "square up" the short end of the strip. Place the short side of the ruler along the top of the strip. Square up the short side of the strip by cutting approximately 1/4" from the edge.

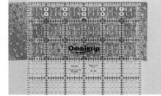

Left-Handed   *Right-Handed*

2. After squaring up one end of the strip, turn the mat one-half turn (180°). Place the ruler on top of the fabric so the 3" marking aligns with the newly cut edge. Be sure the top of the ruler is even with the top of the strip. Firmly hold the ruler with one hand and cut along the edge of the ruler with your rotary cutter.

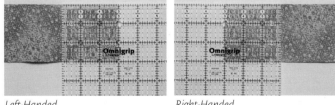

Left-Handed   *Right-Handed*

Cutting a Rectangle

The cutting chart for each block gives the cut dimensions for the rectangles. Use the smaller dimension to determine the width of the strip you will cut. Let's say the cutting instructions call for two 3" x 5" rectangles. Cut a 3" x 11" strip of fabric; this allows an extra inch for squaring up.

Square up the short end of the strip as in Step 1 for cutting a square. Turn the mat one-half turn. Next, place the ruler on top of the strip so the 5" marking aligns with the newly cut edge. Be sure the top of the ruler is even with the top of the strip. Rotary cut.

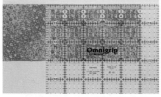
Left-Handed

Right-Handed

SEWING

Sewing perfect Eight-Pointed Star blocks has never been easier! No more back-tacking, set-in seams, or bias edges to deal with. Straight sewing is all that's required.

In this section, I share some of my special hints and tips for making perfect stars. By following these suggestions, you will avoid common problems that may occur when working with squares and rectangles.

Seam Allowance

I find it's best to use a scant $1/4$" seam allowance when piecing quilts. Using a scant seam allowance ensures the units and blocks are true to size because you regain the small amount of fabric that is lost due to the thickness of the sewing thread and the resulting "hump" that's created by pressing the seam allowances to one side.

Sewing on the Diagonal Using Two Layered Squares

This quick and easy method uses two squares of equal size to create one or two half-square triangles.

NO-FAIL TIPS FOR SEWING ON THE DIAGONAL

Follow these hints for sewing diagonal seams, and you will get perfect piecing results every time.

■ When working with squares and rectangles, sometimes you need to draw a thin, diagonal pencil line through the piece in order to sew it to the next piece. *Do not* sew precisely on the drawn pencil line. You should sew one or two thread widths to the right of it to obtain a scant $1/4$" seam allowance. This ensures the piece will be the correct size after pressing. If you sew exactly on the pencil line, the piece will likely be too small after pressing.

Pencil line →

— Sewing line

Stitch just to the right of the pencil line

■ Use a mechanical pencil with a lead no more than 0.5mm in diameter for drawing diagonal lines on light fabric, and use a black Ultra Fine Point Sharpie for dark fabrics. Do not use a regular pencil. It will become dull very quickly, and the pencil line will be wider and bolder than desired.

■ Keep sharp needles in your sewing machine. A dull needle will distort the first few stitches. I use a 70/10 Jeans/Denim needle by Schmetz for all of my machine piecing.

■ A single hole or straight stitch plate is also helpful. It keeps the needle from pushing the corner of the square into the zigzag throat plate hole (which has a larger opening).

■ When sewing diagonally through a square or rectangle, start sewing on a scrap piece of fabric first, then con-

tinue sewing into the adjacent square/rectangle. This will help prevent distortion of the first one or two stitches.

■ Try piecing with an open-toe walking foot. This will allow you to see where to sew *next* to the pencil line. I do all of my machine piecing on a Bernina with an open-toe walking foot.

■ The needle-stop down feature on my sewing machine is very helpful when chain piecing. It keeps the fabric in place when you stop sewing momentarily. Use this feature if your machine has it.

■ Press the diagonally sewn seam flat to "set" the stitches. This prevents distortion of the seam and pieces. Next press the seam allowance to one side, then trim off the excess fabric.

HOW TO CREATE ONE PIECED SQUARE

Begin with two same-size squares cut as directed for the block you are making.

1. Draw a diagonal line on the wrong side of one square, usually the lighter color. With right sides together, place that square on top of the other square. Stitch one or two thread widths to the right of the pencil line. Press the square according to the pressing arrows in the block instructions.

2. Carefully place the pieces on a cutting mat. Using a ruler and rotary cutter, cut ¼" away from the stitching line. You will have two triangle-shaped pieces of fabric left over. Discard these pieces or save them for future projects.

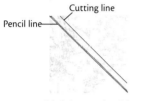

*Stitch just to the right
of the pencil line.*

HOW TO CREATE TWO PIECED SQUARES

Begin with two same-size squares cut as directed for the block you are making.

1. Draw a diagonal line from corner to corner on the wrong side of the lighter square. Next draw a diagonal line ¼" away from and parallel to the first diagonal line. Do the same on the opposite side of the first diagonal line. With right sides together, position the lighter square on top of the darker square.

Draw pencil lines ¼" apart and parallel to each other.

2. Sew one or two thread widths on the inside of the outermost pencil lines. Using a ruler and rotary cutter, cut along the center diagonal pencil line. Press.

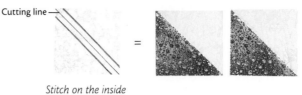

*Stitch on the inside
of the pencil line.*

SEW MAGIC

Try Omnigrid's new Diamond-Free Omnigrip ruler to trim the ¼" seam allowance more easily and quickly than you ever thought possible. The highlighted ¼" vertical area on the ruler will eliminate any cutting errors. It will also work great when you need to draw stitching lines exactly ¼" away from a diagonal line when creating two pieced squares (see Step 1 below left).

SEWING ON THE DIAGONAL USING A SQUARE AND A RECTANGLE

1. On the wrong side of the fabric, draw a diagonal line across the square. With right sides together, place the square on the rectangle. Stitch one or two thread widths to the right of the pencil line.

2. Press the square according to the pressing arrows in the block instructions. Carefully place the pieces on a cutting mat and fold the square back. Using a ruler and rotary cutter, trim ¼" away from the stitching line. You will have two triangle-shaped pieces of fabric left over.

Trim ¼" from the stitching line.

SEWING ON THE DIAGONAL USING TWO RECTANGLES

1. In order to draw a pencil line on a rectangle, position the top rectangle a little away from the edge of the rectangle that is beneath it.

Align the top edge of the upper rectangle with the top edge of the lower rectangle. This allows you to see where to draw the diagonal pencil line. Draw a diagonal pencil line from the upper corner to where the rectangles meet (45° angle).

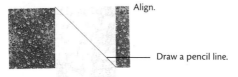

Align.

Draw a pencil line.

2. Move the top rectangle so the edges of the two rectangles are even. Sew, press, and trim ¼" from the stitching line.

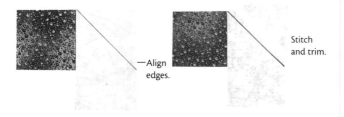

Align edges.

Stitch and trim.

FABRIC AND THREAD CHOICES

I've used good quality, 100% cotton fabric for the blocks and quilts in this book. I prefer to work with cottons, but that doesn't mean you have to. The Diamond-Free method will work equally well with other types of fabrics too. If possible, prewash the fabrics before using them. This ensures that the fabrics are preshrunk and the dyes won't bleed if your block or quilt must be washed in the future.

All of my machine piecing is done with Mettler 100% cotton, silk-finish thread. The weight is 50/3. For most of my piecing, I use a light beige color thread (color #703 or #810).

NO-FAIL PRESSING TIPS

■ Be sure to press each seam allowance before continuing to sew more pieces to the unit.

■ I've included pressing arrows with the block instructions. These are highly recommended pressing suggestions. If you follow these pressing arrows, you should be able to butt most of your pieces together to accurately align and stitch them together. This will help keep your blocks square.

■ I normally don't use steam when piecing. I find it tends to distort many of the smaller pieces. Be extra careful if you use steam while pressing.

■ Use the cotton setting on your iron. If this doesn't seem hot enough, set it one notch higher. After pressing a piece, it should lie fairly flat on the ironing board. If it doesn't, it's a sure sign that the iron isn't hot enough.

■ To get stubborn seam allowances to lie flat, place a tiny piece of ¼" wide Steam-a-Seam 2 under the seam allowance and press. This will fuse the seam allowance in place.

Diamond-Free® METHOD

Making star blocks couldn't get any easier once you sew them the Diamond-Free way. This patented method is based upon separating any eight-pointed star into eight units: four Unit 1s and four Unit 2s. Unit 2s are mirror images of Unit 1s. The same letter (A, B, C) is used to identify identical pieces in each unit.

When Unit 1 is positioned next to Unit 2, a quarter of a star is formed. Four of these quarter units create a full star.

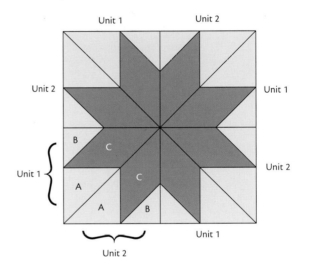

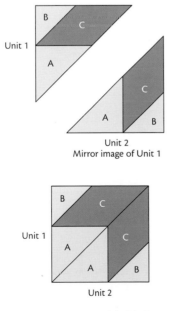

Unit 1

Unit 2
Mirror image of Unit 1

One quarter of the block

Even though A and B appear as half-square triangles and C appears as a 45° diamond, only squares and rectangles are used! Keep reading if you don't believe me.

The following step-by-step photos will show you how easy it is to make a basic Eight-Pointed Star and a Lone Star using the Diamond-Free method. All the blocks in the book are sewn much the same way, with simple variations. Each block includes cutting dimensions for several different sizes, along with step-by-step sewing instructions.

EIGHT-POINTED STAR, *BLOCK 1*

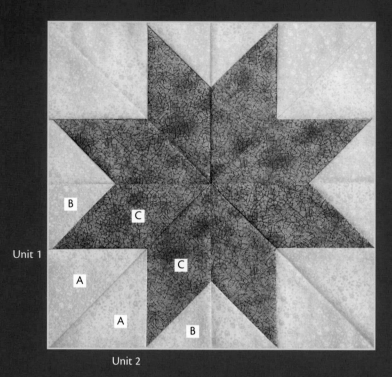

Unit 1

Unit 2

FOR THIS BLOCK YOU NEED TO CUT:

8 rectangles for A

8 squares for B

8 rectangles for C

The following photos are of Block 1 (page 18), an Eight-Pointed Star.

1. On the wrong side of the fabric, draw a diagonal line on all B squares.

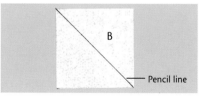

2. Unit 1—With right sides together, position a B square on the lower part of a C rectangle, making sure the diagonal pencil line starts in the upper left corner. Four Unit 1s are required.

Unit 2—With right sides together, position a B square on the lower part of a C rectangle, making sure the diagonal pencil line starts in the upper right corner. Four Unit 2s are required.

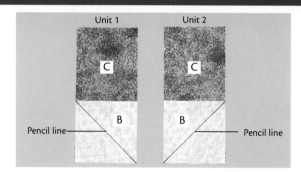

3. Stitch one or two thread widths to the right of the pencil line (the C rectangle is to your left when sewing). Press according to the arrows. Fold the fabric back and trim ¼" away from the stitching line. Discard the cutoff triangles. Repeat for a total of four Unit 1s and four Unit 2s.

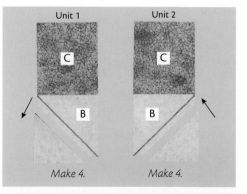

Make 4.   Make 4.

4. Unit 1—Sew an A rectangle to the right side of the B/C unit. Press toward the B/C unit. Repeat this on all four Unit 1s.

Unit 2—Sew an A rectangle to the left side of the B/C unit. Press toward A. Repeat this on all four Unit 2s.

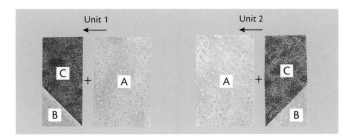

5. On the WRONG SIDE of all Unit 2s, draw a diagonal pencil line from the upper left corner to the lower right corner.

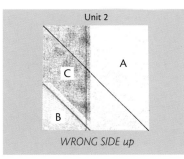

WRONG SIDE up

6. With the RIGHT SIDES of Unit 1 and Unit 2 facing each other, place Unit 2 on top of Unit 1. Align the pieces and pin to secure. Repeat this step for a total of four sets.

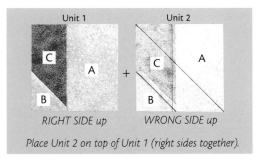

RIGHT SIDE up   *WRONG SIDE up*

Place Unit 2 on top of Unit 1 (right sides together).

7. On the WRONG SIDE of all Unit 2s, sew one or two thread widths to the right of the pencil line. Press according to the arrow and trim ¼" away from the stitching line. Discard the cutoff triangles or save for another project.

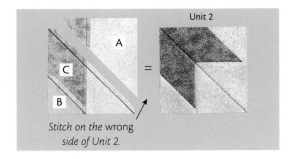

Stitch on the wrong side of Unit 2.

8. With the RIGHT SIDES facing each other, sew a Unit 1–2 set to another Unit 1–2 set. Press according to the arrow. Make two sets.

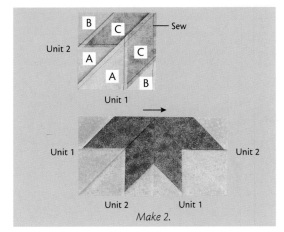

Make 2.

9. With the RIGHT SIDES of each half-star facing each other, align, pin, and sew together.

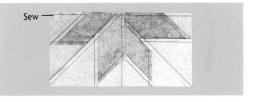

Congratulations! You've now sewn an Eight-Pointed Star the Diamond-Free way.

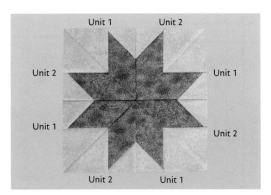

LONE STAR, *BLOCK 9*

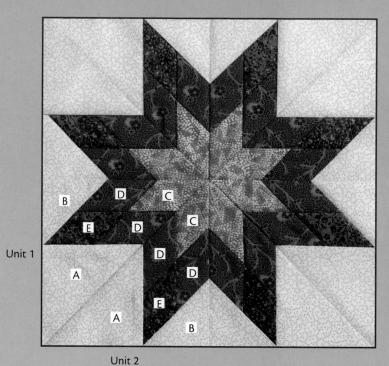

Unit 1

Unit 2

FOR THIS BLOCK YOU NEED TO CUT:

8 rectangles for A

8 squares for B

8 rectangles for C

16 rectangles for D

8 rectangles for E

The Eight-Pointed Star was only the beginning! Once I discovered how easily the Diamond-Free method worked for that block, I quickly began investigating how I could use this method for other stars. The second example is a Lone Star, Block 9 (page 34). The photos that follow show how easily a Lone Star can be sewn with only squares and rectangles. Remember, simply separate the star into four Unit 1s and four Unit 2s and label the pieces within each unit.

One quarter of the star is formed when Unit 1 is sewn together with Unit 2. Four of these quarters are needed to complete the Lone Star.

A and B appear as half-square triangles. C, D, and E appear as 45° diamonds. But as before, you will see how only squares and rectangles are needed to create a perfect Lone Star.

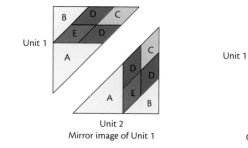

Unit 2
Mirror image of Unit 1

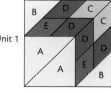

Unit 2
One quarter of the block

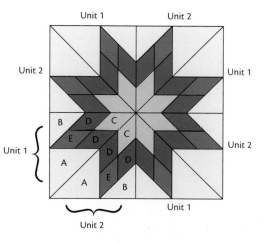

1. Draw a diagonal line on the wrong side of all B squares.

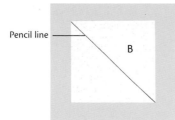

Pencil line — B

2. Refer to page 10 for Sewing on the Diagonal Using Two Rectangles. Draw a 45° diagonal pencil line on the wrong side of the D rectangles. Remember that Unit 2 is a mirror image of Unit 1, which means the pencil lines will be facing in the opposite direction. With right sides together, place the D rectangle on the C rectangle. Stitch one or two thread widths to the right of the pencil line. Press according to the arrow. Trim ¼" away from the stitching line. Discard the cutoff triangles. Repeat for a total of four sets of Unit 1 and four sets of Unit 2.

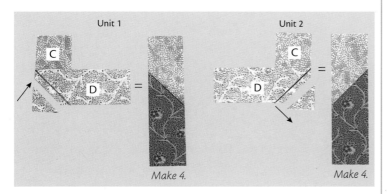

Unit 1 — C D — Make 4.
Unit 2 — C D — Make 4.

3. Draw a 45° diagonal pencil line on the wrong side of rectangle E. With right sides together, place the E rectangle on the D rectangle. Stitch, press and trim as in Step 2. Repeat for a total of four sets of Unit 1 and four sets of Unit 2.

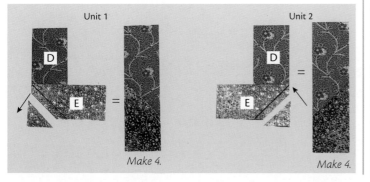

Unit 1 — D E — Make 4.
Unit 2 — D E — Make 4.

4. **Unit 1**— Sew strip C/D to strip D/E. Make four.
Unit 2— Sew strip C/D to strip D/E. Make four.

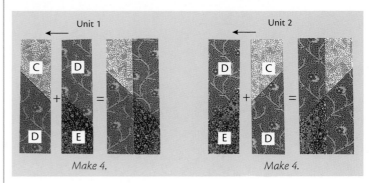

Unit 1 — C D + D E — Make 4.
Unit 2 — D C + E D — Make 4.

5. **Unit 1**— With right sides together, position a B square on the lower part of the C/D/E set. Make sure the diagonal pencil line starts in the upper left corner of B. Stitch, press, and trim. After sewing the B square, add an A rectangle to the right side. Press according to the arrow. Make four Unit 1s.

Unit 2— With right sides together, position a B square on the lower part of the C/D/E set. Make sure the diagonal pencil line starts in the upper right corner of B. Stitch, press, and trim. After sewing the B square, add an A rectangle to the left side. Press according to the arrow. Make four Unit 2s.

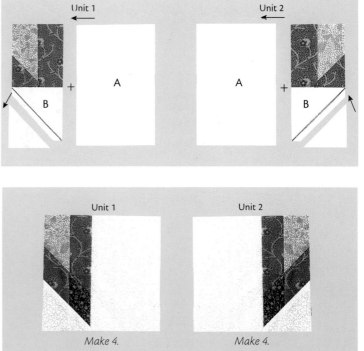

Unit 1 — B + A
Unit 2 — A + B

Unit 1 — Make 4.
Unit 2 — Make 4.

6. On the WRONG SIDE of all Unit 2s, draw a diagonal pencil line from the upper left corner to the lower right corner.

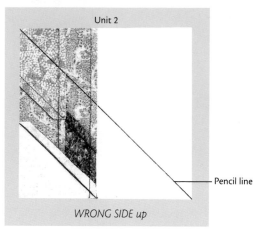

Unit 2

Pencil line

WRONG SIDE up

7. With the RIGHT SIDES of Unit 1 and Unit 2 facing each other, place Unit 2 on top of Unit 1. Align the pieces together and pin to secure. Repeat to make a total of four sets.

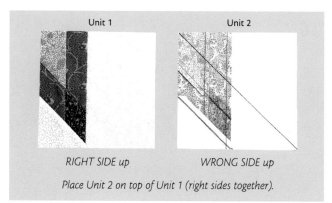

Unit 1   Unit 2

RIGHT SIDE up   *WRONG SIDE up*

Place Unit 2 on top of Unit 1 (right sides together).

8. On the WRONG SIDE of all Unit 2s, sew one or two thread widths to the right of the pencil line. Press according to the arrow and trim ¼" away from the stitching line. Discard the cutoff triangles or save for another project.

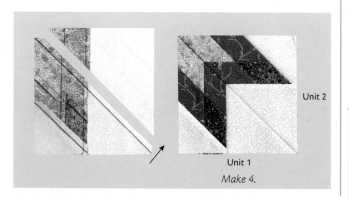

Unit 2

Unit 1

Make 4.

9. With the RIGHT SIDES facing each other, sew a Unit 1–2 set to another Unit 1–2 set. Press according to the arrow. Make two sets.

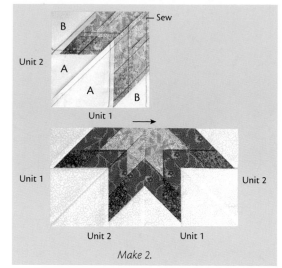

B   Sew

Unit 2

A

A   B

Unit 1

Unit 1   Unit 2

Unit 2   Unit 1

Make 2.

10. With the RIGHT SIDES of each half-star facing each other, align, pin, and sew together.

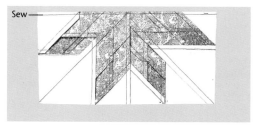

Sew

Now you've sewn a Lone Star block without cutting a single diamond!

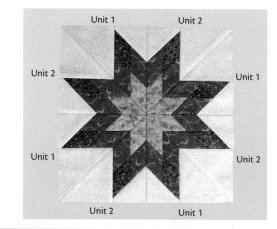

Unit 1   Unit 2

Unit 2   Unit 1

Unit 1   Unit 2

Unit 2   Unit 1

SEW MAGIC
For blocks 6" and smaller, trim the seam allowances a scant ¼". This will reduce the bulk after pressing and make the finished block look flatter.

How to Read **THE CHARTS**

Letters refer to specific pieces in the block illustration.

Color as it appears in the featured block.

Number of squares or rectangles to cut.

Finished block sizes to choose from.

USED FOR	COLOR	NUMBER TO CUT	BLOCK SIZE				
			4"	5"	6"	7"	8"
A		8	1⅝ x 2½	2 x 3	2¼ x 3½	2½ x 4	2⅞ x 4½
B		8	1⅜	1½	1¾	2	2⅛
C		8	1⅜ x 2½	1½ x 3	1¾ x 3½	2 x 4	2⅛ x 4½

Sizes to cut in inches.

Blocks

The cutting charts for the individual blocks list the cut size of each piece, in inches. Single measurements indicate the size of a cut square (3 = 3" x 3").

Quilt Maps

Yardage and Cutting charts are provided with each quilt map. I've overestimated the yardage needed by a small amount to allow for preshrinking the fabric and squaring up. For the blocks, you should have more than enough fabric, even if you decide to cut half of the pieces on the crosswise grain and half on the lengthwise grain (see Using Directional Fabrics, page 82). All yardage is based on 40" of useable width.

Some fabrics are used in both the block(s) and the quilt map. For the total amount of each fabric needed, add the same-color quantities together.

I've included the exact measurements for cutting borders, but it's best to measure your quilt top before cutting border strips. Most borders are cut crosswise and are pieced when longer than 40". If you want to cut borders lengthwise, buy extra fabric as needed.

I allowed 3" strips when cutting binding even though I usually cut 2⅛" strips for double-fold binding. The backing is 6" larger than the size of the quilt.

Letters refer to specific pieces of the quilt map

Color as it appears in the featured quilt

Yardage needed

YARDAGE

ITEM	COLOR	QUANTITY NEEDED
A		¼ yard
*B		½ yard
C		⅜ yard
*D, *E		1⅛ yard
*Binding		½ yard
Backing		55" x 55"

Based on cutting crosswise grain of the fabric.

CUTTING

ITEM	COLOR	# TO CUT	SIZE	
A		36	1¾" x 1¾"	◻
B		24	1¾" x 10½"	
C		8	11¾" x 11¾"	⊠
D		2	6" x 38"	
*E		4	6" x 24¾"	

Piece two border strips together for the required length.

◻ Indicates to cut each square in half diagonally once to make two triangles.

⊠ Indicates to cut each square in half diagonally twice to make four triangles.

Block 1

USED FOR	COLOR	NUMBER TO CUT	**BLOCK SIZE**				
			4"	5"	6"	7"	8"
A		8	1⅝ x 2½	2 x 3	2¼ x 3½	2½ x 4	2⅞ x 4½
B		8	1⅜	1½	1¾	2	2⅛
C		8	1⅜ x 2½	1½ x 3	1¾ x 3½	2 x 4	2⅛ x 4½
			9"	10"	11"	12"	13"
A		8	3⅛ x 5	3½ x 5½	3¾ x 6	4 x 6½	4¼ x 7
B		8	2⅜	2½	2¾	3	3¼
C		8	2⅜ x 5	2½ x 5½	2¾ x 6	3 x 6½	3¼ x 7
			14"	15"	16"	17"	18"
A		8	4⅝ x 7½	4⅞ x 8	5¼ x 8½	5½ x 9	5¾ x 9½
B		8	3⅜	3⅝	3¾	4	4¼
C		8	3⅜ x 7½	3⅝ x 8	3¾ x 8½	4 x 9	4¼ x 9½

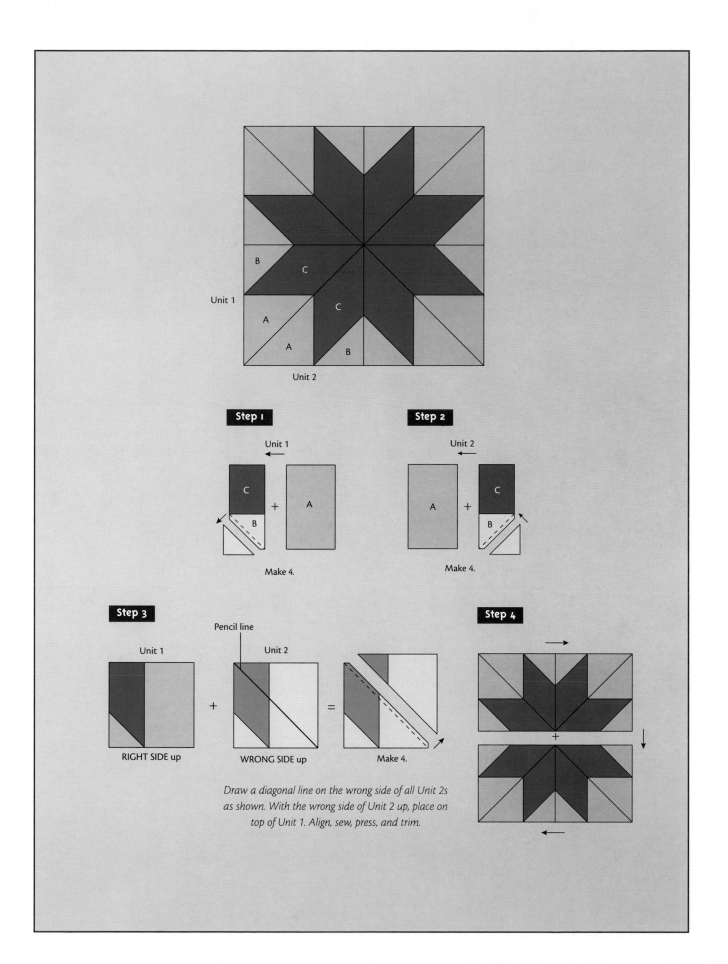

Unit 1

Unit 2

Step 1

Unit 1

C
B

+

A

Make 4.

Step 2

Unit 2

A

+

C
B

Make 4.

Step 3

Unit 1

Pencil line

Unit 2

+

=

Make 4.

RIGHT SIDE up

WRONG SIDE up

Step 4

+

Draw a diagonal line on the wrong side of all Unit 2s as shown. With the wrong side of Unit 2 up, place on top of Unit 1. Align, sew, press, and trim.

Block 2

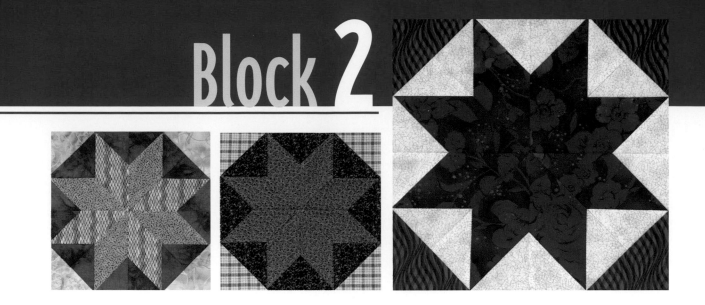

BLOCK SIZE

USED FOR	COLOR	NUMBER TO CUT	4"	6"	8"	9"	10"
A	⬜	8	1⅝ x 2½	2¼ x 3½	2⅞ x 4½	3⅛ x 5	3½ x 5½
B	⬜	8	1⅜	1¾	2⅛	2⅜	2½
C	⬛	8	1⅜ x 2½	1¾ x 3½	2⅛ x 4½	2⅜ x 5	2½ x 5½
D	⬛	4	1⅝	2¼	2⅞	3⅛	3½

USED FOR	COLOR	NUMBER TO CUT	12"	14"	15"	16"	18"
A	⬜	8	4 x 6½	4⅝ x 7½	4⅞ x 8	5¼ x 8½	5¾ x 9½
B	⬜	8	3	3⅜	3⅝	3¾	4¼
C	⬛	8	3 x 6½	3⅜ x 7½	3⅝ x 8	3¾ x 8½	4¼ x 9½
D	⬛	4	4	4⅝	4⅞	5¼	5¾

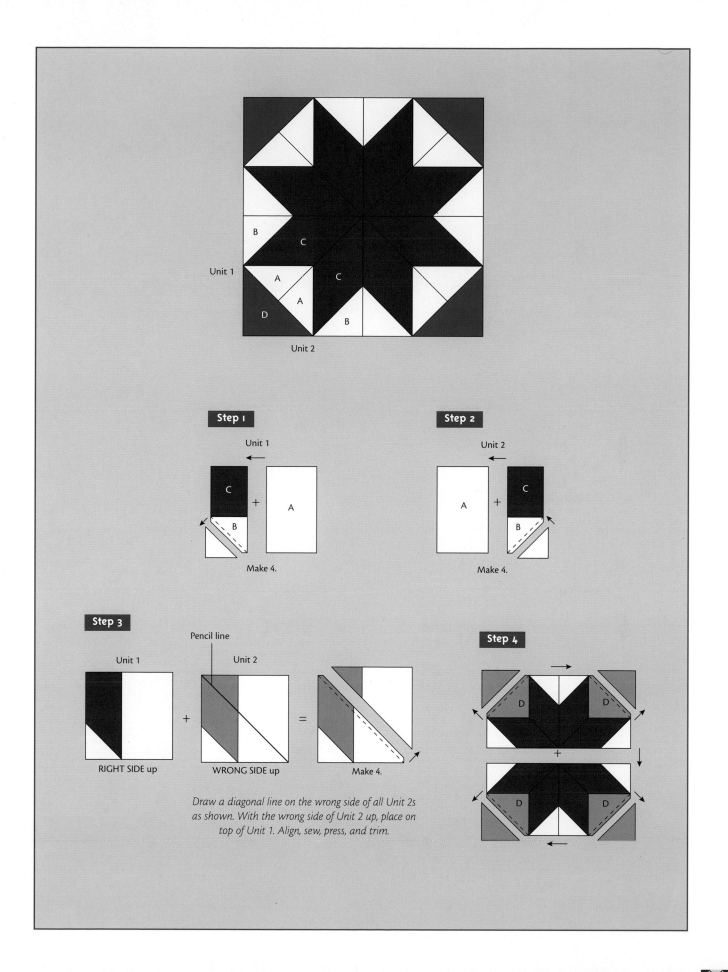

Unit 1

C

B

A

A

D

C

C

B

Unit 2

Step 1

Unit 1

C

B

+

A

Make 4.

Step 2

Unit 2

A

+

C

B

Make 4.

Step 3

Pencil line

Unit 1

Unit 2

+

=

RIGHT SIDE up

WRONG SIDE up

Make 4.

Draw a diagonal line on the wrong side of all Unit 2s as shown. With the wrong side of Unit 2 up, place on top of Unit 1. Align, sew, press, and trim.

Step 4

D

D

+

D

D

Block 3

BLOCK SIZE

USED FOR	COLOR	NUMBER TO CUT	4"	6"	8"	9"	10"
A	(white)	4	1⅝ x 2½	2¼ x 3½	2⅞ x 4½	3⅛ x 5	3½ x 5½
B	(white)	8	1⅜	1¾	2⅛	2⅜	2½
C	(white)	4	1⅝	2¼	2⅞	3⅛	3½
D	(gray)	8	1⅜ x 2½	1¾ x 3½	2⅛ x 4½	2⅜ x 5	2½ x 5½
E	(black)	4	1⅝ x 2½	2¼ x 3½	2⅞ x 4½	3⅛ x 5	3½ x 5½
F	(black)	4	1⅝	2¼	2⅞	3⅛	3½

			12"	14"	15"	16"	18"
A	(white)	4	4 x 6½	4⅝ x 7½	4⅞ x 8	5¼ x 8½	5¾ x 9½
B	(white)	8	3	3⅜	3⅝	3¾	4¼
C	(white)	4	4	4⅝	4⅞	5¼	5¾
D	(gray)	8	3 x 6½	3⅜ x 7½	3⅝ x 8	3¾ x 8½	4¼ x 9½
E	(black)	4	4 x 6½	4⅝ x 7½	4⅞ x 8	5¼ x 8½	5¾ x 9½
F	(black)	4	4	4⅝	4⅞	5¼	5¾

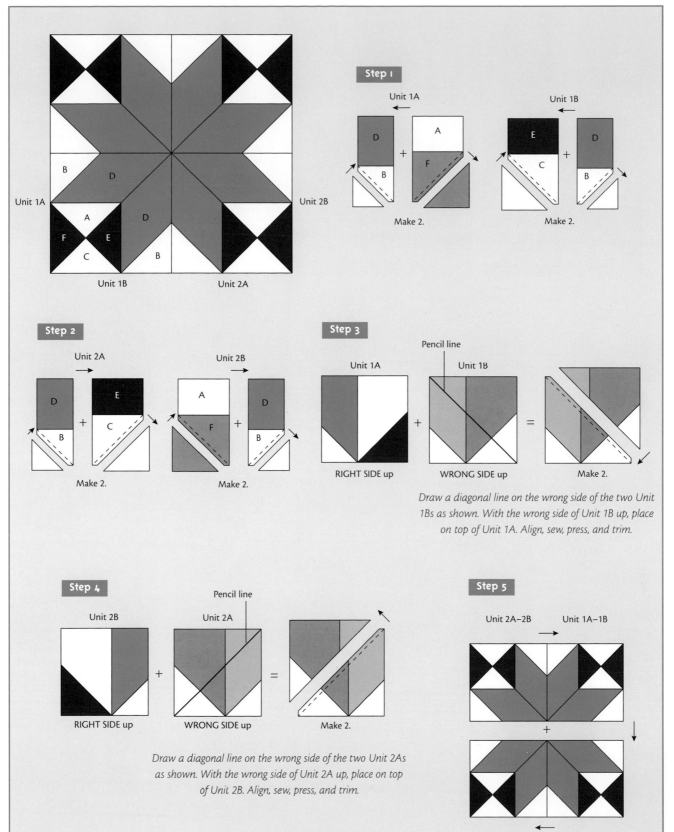

Step 1

Unit 1A

D + A / F / B   Make 2.

Unit 1B

E / D + C / B   Make 2.

Step 2

Unit 2A

D + E / C / B   Make 2.

Unit 2B

A / F + D / B   Make 2.

Step 3

Unit 1A
RIGHT SIDE up

Pencil line

Unit 1B
WRONG SIDE up

=

Make 2.

Draw a diagonal line on the wrong side of the two Unit 1Bs as shown. With the wrong side of Unit 1B up, place on top of Unit 1A. Align, sew, press, and trim.

Step 4

Unit 2B
RIGHT SIDE up

Pencil line

Unit 2A
WRONG SIDE up

=

Make 2.

Draw a diagonal line on the wrong side of the two Unit 2As as shown. With the wrong side of Unit 2A up, place on top of Unit 2B. Align, sew, press, and trim.

Step 5

Unit 2A–2B   Unit 1A–1B

+

Unit 1A–1B   Unit 2A–2B

Block 4

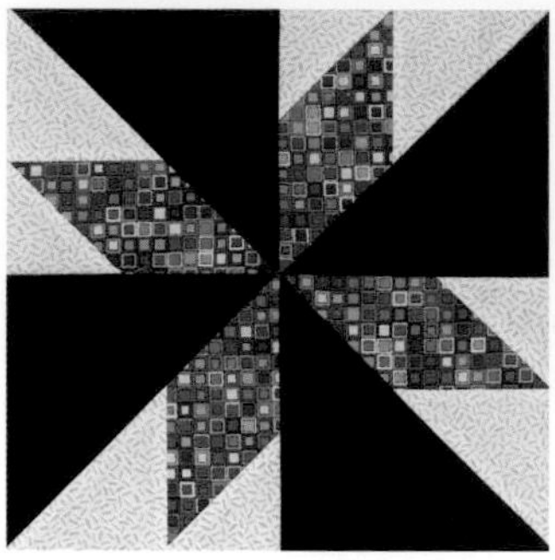

USED FOR	COLOR	NUMBER TO CUT	BLOCK SIZE				
			4"	6"	8"	9"	10"
A		4	1⅝ x 2½	2¼ x 3½	2⅞ x 4½	3⅛ x 5	3½ x 5½
B		4	1⅜	1¾	2⅛	2⅜	2½
C		4	1⅜ x 2½	1¾ x 3½	2⅛ x 4½	2⅜ x 5	2½ x 5½
D		4	2½	3½	4½	5	5½

USED FOR	COLOR	NUMBER TO CUT	12"	14"	15"	16"	18"
A		4	4 x 6½	4⅝ x 7½	4⅞ x 8	5¼ x 8½	5¾ x 9½
B		4	3	3⅜	3⅝	3¾	4¼
C		4	3 x 6½	3⅜ x 7½	3⅝ x 8	3¾ x 8½	4¼ x 9½
D		4	6½	7½	8	8½	9½

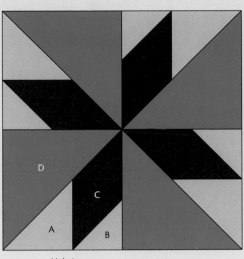

Unit 1

Step 1

Unit 1 ←

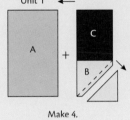

A + C
B

Make 4.

Step 2

Pencil line

Unit 1

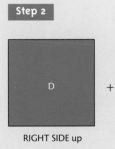 + 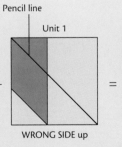 =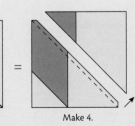

RIGHT SIDE up   WRONG SIDE up   Make 4.

*Draw a diagonal line on the wrong side of all Unit 1s
as shown. With the wrong side of Unit 1 up, place on
top of D. Align, sew, press, and trim.*

Step 3

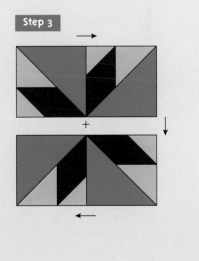

Block 5

			BLOCK SIZE			
USED FOR	COLOR	NUMBER TO CUT	6"	10"	11"	12"
A		8	2¼ x 3⅛	3½ x 5	3¾ x 5⅜	4 x 5¾
B		8	1⅛ x 1¾	1½ x 2½	1⅝ x 2¾	1¾ x 3
C		8	1¾ x 3½	2½ x 5½	2¾ x 6	3 x 6½
D		8	1⅛ x 1¾	1½ x 2½	1⅝ x 2¾	1¾ x 3
E		8	2¼ x 2⅝	3½ x 4	3¾ x 4⅜	4 x 4¾

USED FOR	COLOR	NUMBER TO CUT	16"	17"	18"
A		8	5¼ x 7⅝	5½ x 8	5¾ x 8⅜
B		8	2⅛ x 3¾	2¼ x 4	2⅜ x 4¼
C		8	3¾ x 8½	4 x 9	4¼ x 9½
D		8	2⅛ x 3¾	2¼ x 4	2⅜ x 4¼
E		8	5¼ x 6⅛	5½ x 6½	5¾ x 6⅞

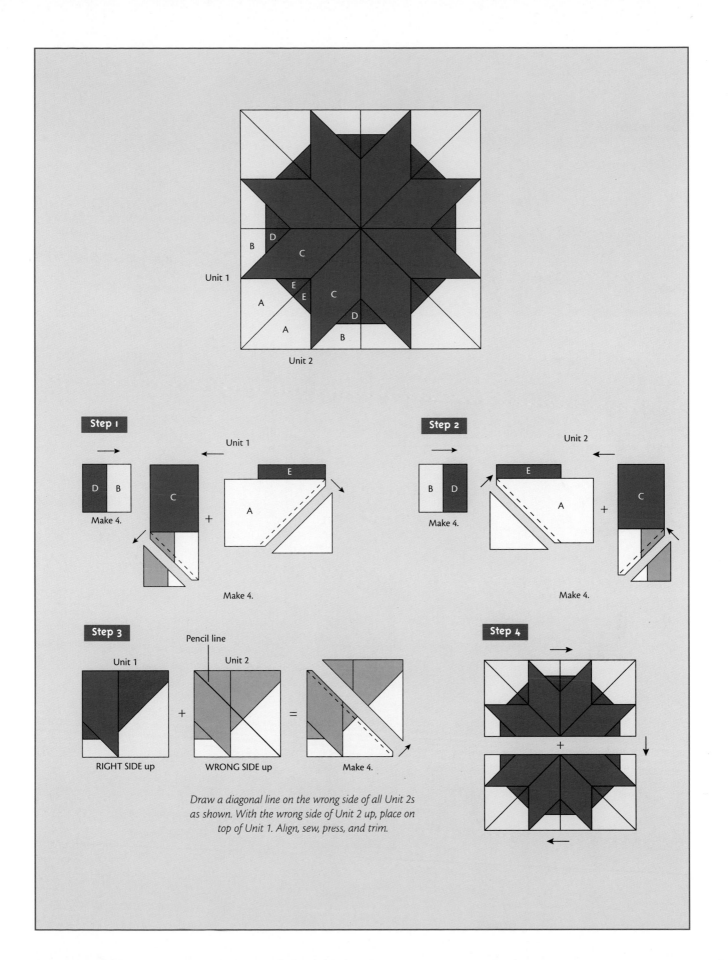

Unit 1

Unit 2

Step 1

Unit 1

D B

Make 4.

C

+

E

A

Make 4.

Step 2

Unit 2

B D

Make 4.

E

A

+

C

Make 4.

Step 3

Unit 1

Pencil line

Unit 2

+

=

Make 4.

RIGHT SIDE up

WRONG SIDE up

*Draw a diagonal line on the wrong side of all Unit 2s
as shown. With the wrong side of Unit 2 up, place on
top of Unit 1. Align, sew, press, and trim.*

Step 4

+

Block 6

USED FOR	COLOR	NUMBER TO CUT	BLOCK SIZE				
			5"	6"	8"	9"	10"
A		8	1¼	1⅜	1⅝	1¾	2
B		8	1½	1¾	2⅛	2⅜	2½
C		8	1½ x 3	1¾ x 3½	2⅛ x 4½	2⅜ x 5	2½ x 5½
D		8	2 x 3	2¼ x 3½	2⅞ x 4½	3⅛ x 5	3½ x 5½

USED FOR	COLOR	NUMBER TO CUT	12"	14"	15"	16"	18"
A		8	2¼	2½	2¾	2⅞	3⅛
B		8	3	3⅜	3⅝	3¾	4¼
C		8	3 x 6½	3⅜ x 7½	3⅝ x 8	3¾ x 8½	4¼ x 9½
D		8	4 x 6½	4⅝ x 7½	4⅞ x 8	5¼ x 8½	5¾ x 9½

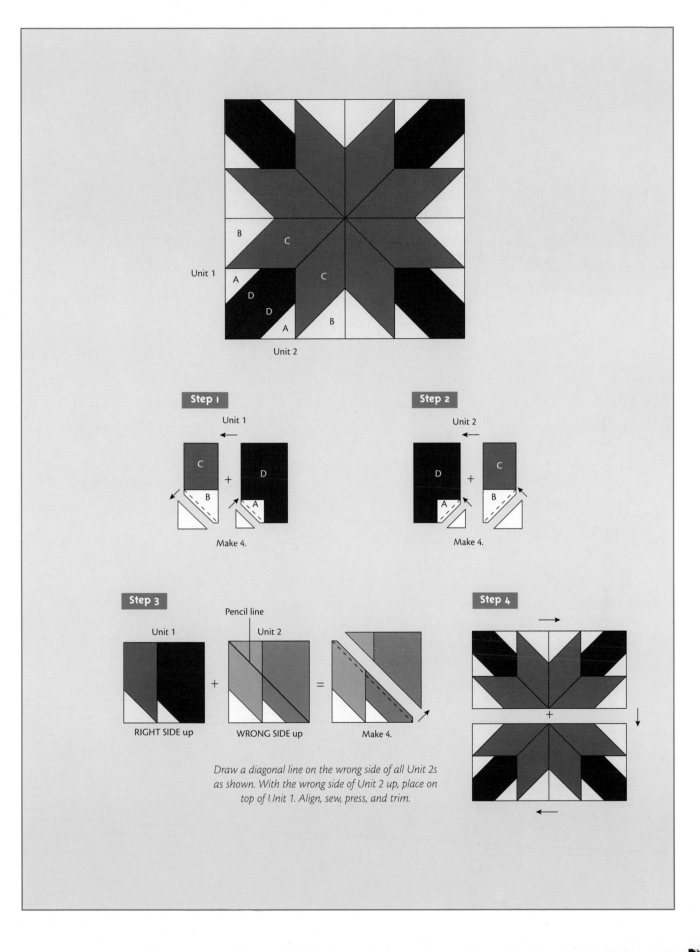

Step 1

Unit 1

Make 4.

Step 2

Unit 2

Make 4.

Step 3

Pencil line

Unit 1

Unit 2

RIGHT SIDE up

WRONG SIDE up

Make 4.

Step 4

Draw a diagonal line on the wrong side of all Unit 2s as shown. With the wrong side of Unit 2 up, place on top of Unit 1. Align, sew, press, and trim.

Block 7

USED FOR	COLOR	NUMBER TO CUT	BLOCK SIZE			
			6"	10"	11"	12"
A		8	2¼ x 3½	3½ x 5½	3¾ x 6	4 x 6½
B		8	1¾	2½	2¾	3
C		4	1¾ x 3½	2½ x 5½	2¾ x 6	3 x 6½
D		8	1⅛ x 2	1½ x 3	1⅝ x 3¼	1¾ x 3½
E		8	1⅛ x 2⅝	1½ x 4	1⅝ x 4⅜	1¾ x 4¾

USED FOR	COLOR	NUMBER TO CUT	16"	17"	18"
A		8	5¼ x 8½	5½ x 9	5¾ x 9½
B		8	3¾	4	4¼
C		4	3¾ x 8½	4 x 9	4¼ x 9½
D		8	2⅛ x 4½	2¼ x 4¾	2⅜ x 5
E		8	2⅛ x 6⅛	2¼ x 6½	2⅜ x 6⅞

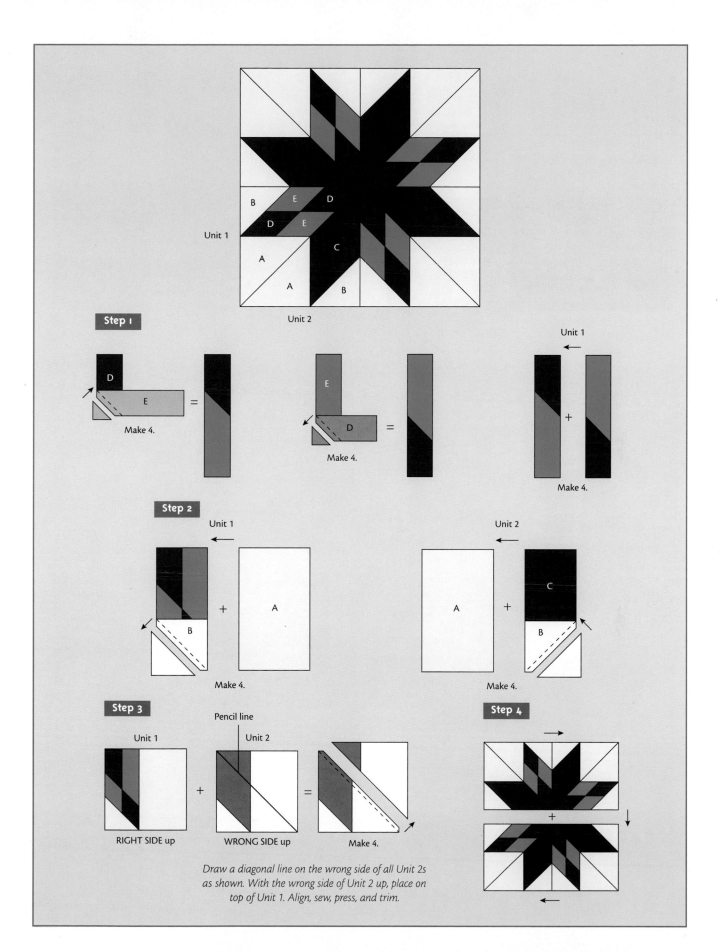

Step 1

Make 4.

Make 4.

Unit 1

Make 4.

Step 2

Unit 1

+ A

B

Make 4.

Unit 2

A + C

B

Make 4.

Step 3

Unit 1   Pencil line   Unit 2

+   =

RIGHT SIDE up   WRONG SIDE up   Make 4.

Draw a diagonal line on the wrong side of all Unit 2s as shown. With the wrong side of Unit 2 up, place on top of Unit 1. Align, sew, press, and trim.

Step 4

+

Block 8

				BLOCK SIZE		
USED FOR	COLOR	NUMBER TO CUT	6"	10"	11"	12"
A		8	2¼ x 3½	3½ x 5½	3¾ x 6	4 x 6½
B		8	1¾	2½	2¾	3
C		8	1⅛ x 3½	1½ x 5½	1⅝ x 6	1¾ x 6½
D		8	1⅛ x 2	1½ x 3	1⅝ x 3¼	1¾ x 3½
E		8	1⅛ x 2⅝	1½ x 4	1⅝ x 4⅜	1¾ x 4¾

			16"	17"	18"
A		8	5¼ x 8½	5½ x 9	5¾ x 9½
B		8	3¾	4	4¼
C		8	2⅛ x 8½	2¼ x 9	2⅜ x 9½
D		8	2⅛ x 4½	2¼ x 4¾	2⅜ x 5
E		8	2⅛ x 6⅛	2¼ x 6½	2⅜ x 6⅞

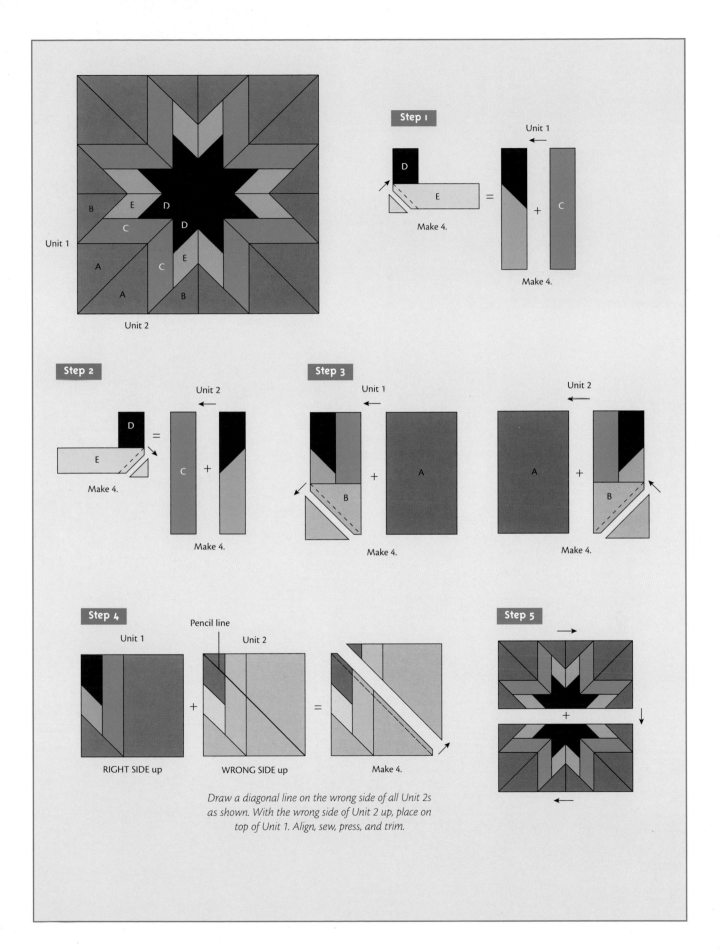

Step 1

Unit 1

Make 4.

= + C

Make 4.

Step 2

Unit 2

D

E

Make 4.

= C +

Make 4.

Step 3

Unit 1

+ A

B

Make 4.

Unit 2

A +

B

Make 4.

Step 4

Unit 1

Pencil line

Unit 2

RIGHT SIDE up + WRONG SIDE up = Make 4.

Draw a diagonal line on the wrong side of all Unit 2s as shown. With the wrong side of Unit 2 up, place on top of Unit 1. Align, sew, press, and trim.

Step 5

+

Block 9

<table>
<tr><th rowspan="2">USED
FOR</th><th rowspan="2">COLOR</th><th rowspan="2">NUMBER
TO CUT</th><th colspan="4">BLOCK SIZE</th></tr>
<tr><th>6"</th><th>10"</th><th>11"</th><th>12"</th></tr>
<tr><td>A</td><td></td><td>8</td><td>2¼ x 3½</td><td>3½ x 5½</td><td>3¾ x 6</td><td>4 x 6½</td></tr>
<tr><td>B</td><td></td><td>8</td><td>1¾</td><td>2½</td><td>2¾</td><td>3</td></tr>
<tr><td>C</td><td></td><td>8</td><td>1⅛ x 2</td><td>1½ x 3</td><td>1⅝ x 3¼</td><td>1¾ x 3½</td></tr>
<tr><td>D</td><td></td><td>16</td><td>1⅛ x 2⅝</td><td>1½ x 4</td><td>1⅝ x 4⅜</td><td>1¾ x 4¾</td></tr>
<tr><td>E</td><td></td><td>8</td><td>1⅛ x 2</td><td>1½ x 3</td><td>1⅝ x 3¼</td><td>1¾ x 3½</td></tr>
</table>

<table>
<tr><th></th><th></th><th></th><th>16"</th><th>17"</th><th>18"</th></tr>
<tr><td>A</td><td></td><td>8</td><td>5¼ x 8½</td><td>5½ x 9</td><td>5¾ x 9½</td></tr>
<tr><td>B</td><td></td><td>8</td><td>3¾</td><td>4</td><td>4¼</td></tr>
<tr><td>C</td><td></td><td>8</td><td>2⅛ x 4½</td><td>2¼ x 4¾</td><td>2⅜ x 5</td></tr>
<tr><td>D</td><td></td><td>16</td><td>2⅛ x 6⅛</td><td>2¼ x 6½</td><td>2⅜ x 6⅞</td></tr>
<tr><td>E</td><td></td><td>8</td><td>2⅛ x 4½</td><td>2¼ x 4¾</td><td>2⅜ x 5</td></tr>
</table>

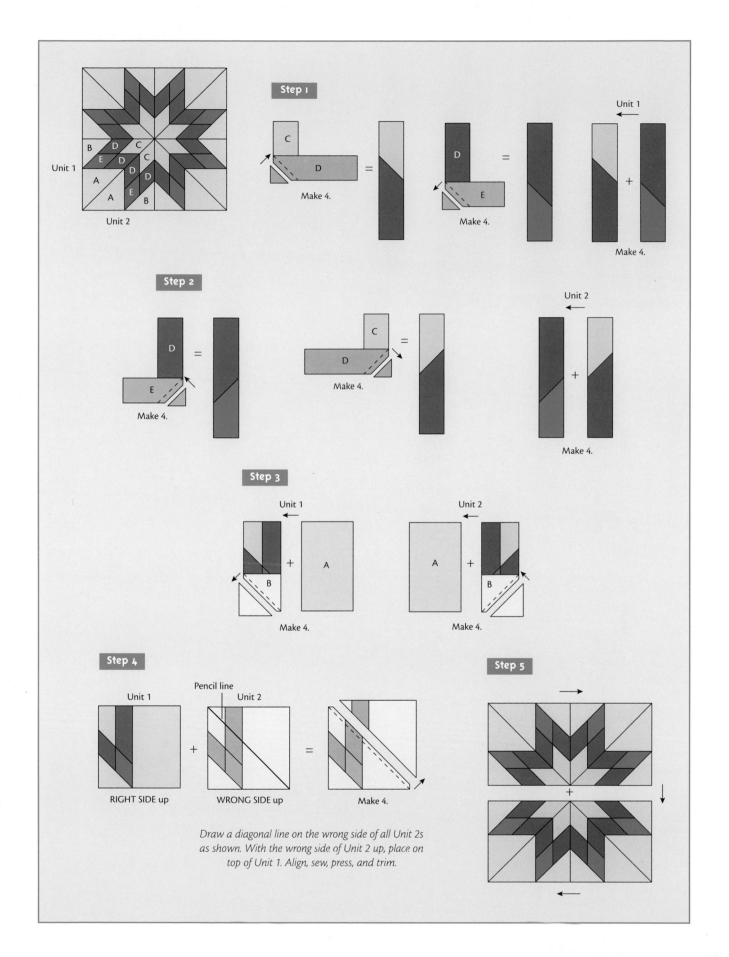

Step 1

Make 4.

Make 4.

Unit 1

Make 4.

Step 2

Make 4.

Make 4.

Unit 2

Make 4.

Step 3

Unit 1

Unit 2

+

A

A

+

B

B

Make 4.

Make 4.

Step 4

Unit 1

Pencil line

Unit 2

+

=

RIGHT SIDE up

WRONG SIDE up

Make 4.

Draw a diagonal line on the wrong side of all Unit 2s as shown. With the wrong side of Unit 2 up, place on top of Unit 1. Align, sew, press, and trim.

Step 5

+

Block 10

USED FOR	COLOR	NUMBER TO CUT	BLOCK SIZE				
			5"	6"	7"	10"	11"
A		8	2 x 3	2¼ x 3½	2½ x 4	3½ x 5½	3¾ x 6
B		8	1½	1¾	2	2½	2¾
C		8	1 x 3	1⅛ x 3½	1¼ x 4	1½ x 5½	1⅝ x 6
D		8	1 x 3	1⅛ x 3½	1¼ x 4	1½ x 5½	1⅝ x 6

USED FOR	COLOR	NUMBER TO CUT	12"	13"	16"	17"	18"
A		8	4 x 6½	4¼ x 7	5¼ x 8½	5½ x 9	5¾ x 9½
B		8	3	3¼	3¾	4	4¼
C		8	1¾ x 6½	1⅞ x 7	2⅛ x 8½	2¼ x 9	2⅜ x 9½
D		8	1¾ x 6½	1⅞ x 7	2⅛ x 8½	2¼ x 9	2⅜ x 9½

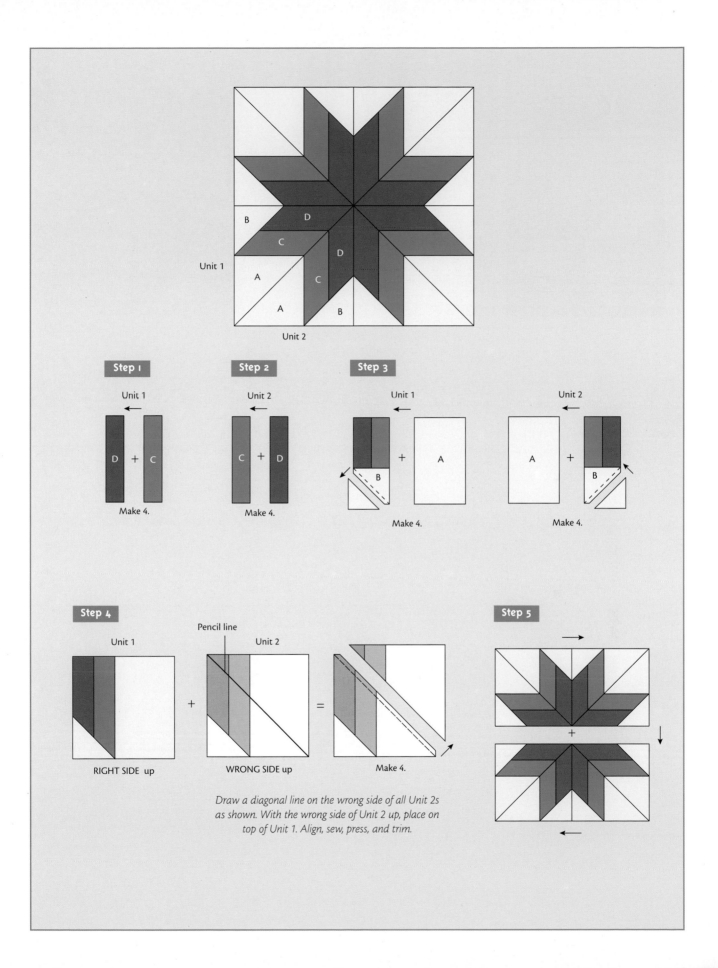

Unit 1

Unit 2

Step 1

Unit 1

D + C

Make 4.

Step 2

Unit 2

C + D

Make 4.

Step 3

Unit 1

B

Make 4.

Unit 2

A + B

Make 4.

Step 4

Pencil line

Unit 1

Unit 2

RIGHT SIDE up

WRONG SIDE up

= Make 4.

Draw a diagonal line on the wrong side of all Unit 2s as shown. With the wrong side of Unit 2 up, place on top of Unit 1. Align, sew, press, and trim.

Step 5

+

Block 11

			BLOCK SIZE				
USED FOR	COLOR	NUMBER TO CUT	5"	6"	7"	10"	11"
A		8	2 x 3	2¼ x 3½	2½ x 4	3½ x 5½	3¾ x 6
B		8	1½	1¾	2	2½	2¾
C		4	1½ x 3	1¾ x 3½	2 x 4	2½ x 5½	2¾ x 6
D		4	1 x 3	1⅛ x 3½	1¼ x 4	1½ x 5½	1⅝ x 6
E		4	1 x 3	1⅛ x 3½	1¼ x 4	1½ x 5½	1⅝ x 6

			12"	13"	16"	17"	18"
A		8	4 x 6½	4¼ x 7	5¼ x 8½	5½ x 9	5¾ x 9½
B		8	3	3¼	3¾	4	4¼
C		4	3 x 6½	3¼ x 7	3¾ x 8½	4 x 9	4¼ x 9½
D		4	1¾ x 6½	1⅞ x 7	2⅛ x 8½	2¼ x 9	2⅜ x 9½
E		4	1¾ x 6½	1⅞ x 7	2⅛ x 8½	2¼ x 9	2⅜ x 9½

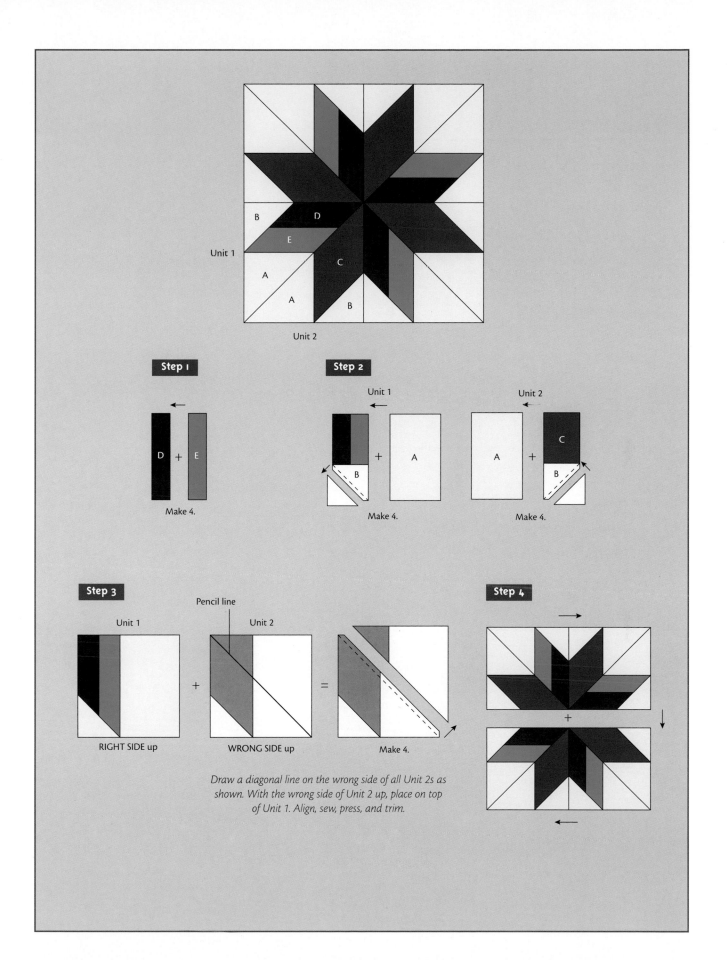

Unit 1

Unit 2

Step 1

D + E

Make 4.

Step 2

Unit 1

B + A

Make 4.

Unit 2

A + C B

Make 4.

Step 3

Pencil line

Unit 1

Unit 2

RIGHT SIDE up   +   WRONG SIDE up   =   Make 4.

Draw a diagonal line on the wrong side of all Unit 2s as shown. With the wrong side of Unit 2 up, place on top of Unit 1. Align, sew, press, and trim.

Step 4

+

Block 12

			BLOCK SIZE				
USED FOR	COLOR	NUMBER TO CUT	6"	8"	9"	10"	11"
A		8	2¼ x 3½	2⅞ x 4½	3⅛ x 5	3½ x 5½	3¾ x 6
B		8	1¾	2⅛	2⅜	2½	2¾
C		4	1¾ x 3½	2⅛ x 4½	2⅜ x 5	2½ x 5½	2¾ x 6
D		4	1¾ x 2¼	2⅛ x 2⅞	2⅜ x 3⅛	2½ x 3½	2¾ x 3¾
E		4	1¾	2⅛	2⅜	2½	2¾
F		4	1¾	2⅛	2⅜	2½	2¾

			12"	14"	15"	16"	18"
A		8	4 x 6½	4⅝ x 7½	4⅞ x 8	5¼ x 8½	5¾ x 9½
B		8	3	3⅜	3⅝	3¾	4¼
C		4	3 x 6½	3⅜ x 7½	3⅝ x 8	3¾ x 8½	4¼ x 9½
D		4	3 x 4	3⅜ x 4⅝	3⅝ x 4⅞	3¾ x 5¼	4¼ x 5¾
E		4	3	3⅜	3⅝	3¾	4¼
F		4	3	3⅜	3⅝	3¾	4¼

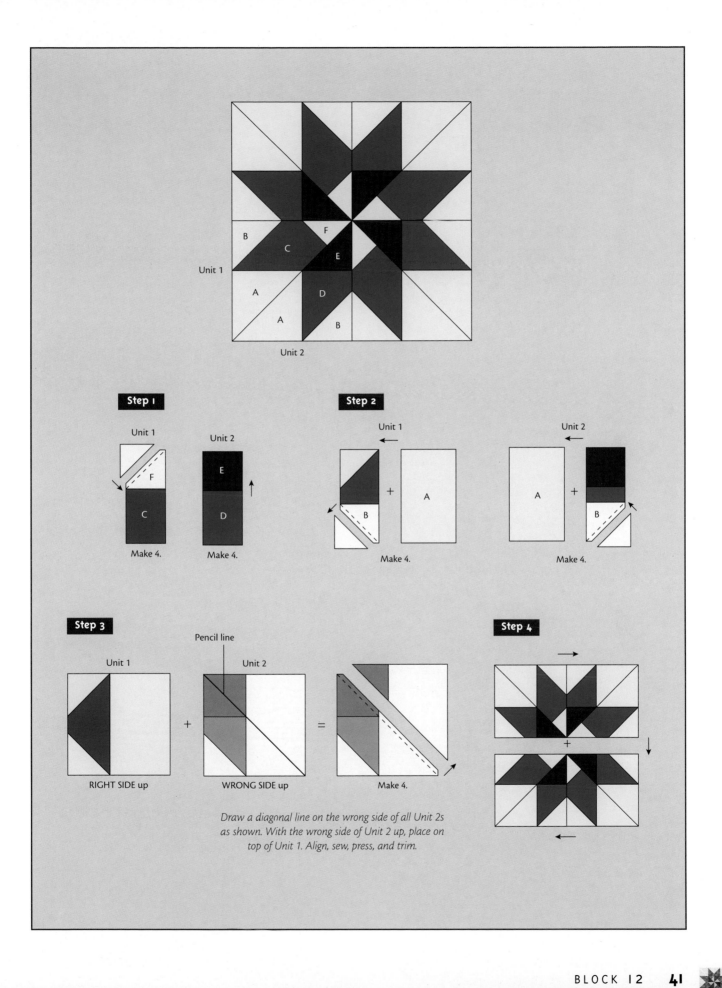

Unit 1

Unit 2

Step 1

Unit 1

F
C

Make 4.

Unit 2

E
D

Make 4.

Step 2

Unit 1

B + A

Make 4.

Unit 2

A + B

Make 4.

Step 3

Pencil line

Unit 1

RIGHT SIDE up

Unit 2

WRONG SIDE up

+ = Make 4.

Draw a diagonal line on the wrong side of all Unit 2s as shown. With the wrong side of Unit 2 up, place on top of Unit 1. Align, sew, press, and trim.

Step 4

+

Block 13

| | | BLOCK SIZE | | | | |
USED FOR	COLOR	NUMBER TO CUT	6"	10"	11"	12"
A		8	2¼ x 3½	3½ x 5½	3¾ x 6	4 x 6½
B		8	1¾	2½	2¾	3
C		4	1⅛ x 3½	1½ x 5½	1⅝ x 6	1¾ x 6½
D		4	1¾ x 2⅝	2½ x 4	2¾ x 4⅜	3 x 4¾
E		4	1⅛ x 3½	1½ x 5½	1⅝ x 6	1¾ x 6½
F		4	1¾ x 2⅝	2½ x 4	2¾ x 4⅜	3 x 4¾

USED FOR	COLOR	NUMBER TO CUT	16"	17"	18"
A		8	5¼ x 8½	5½ x 9	5¾ x 9½
B		8	3¾	4	4¼
C		4	2⅛ x 8½	2¼ x 9	2⅜ x 9½
D		4	3¾ x 6⅛	4 x 6½	4¼ x 6⅞
E		4	2⅛ x 8½	2¼ x 9	2⅜ x 9½
F		4	3¾ x 6⅛	4 x 6½	4¼ x 6⅞

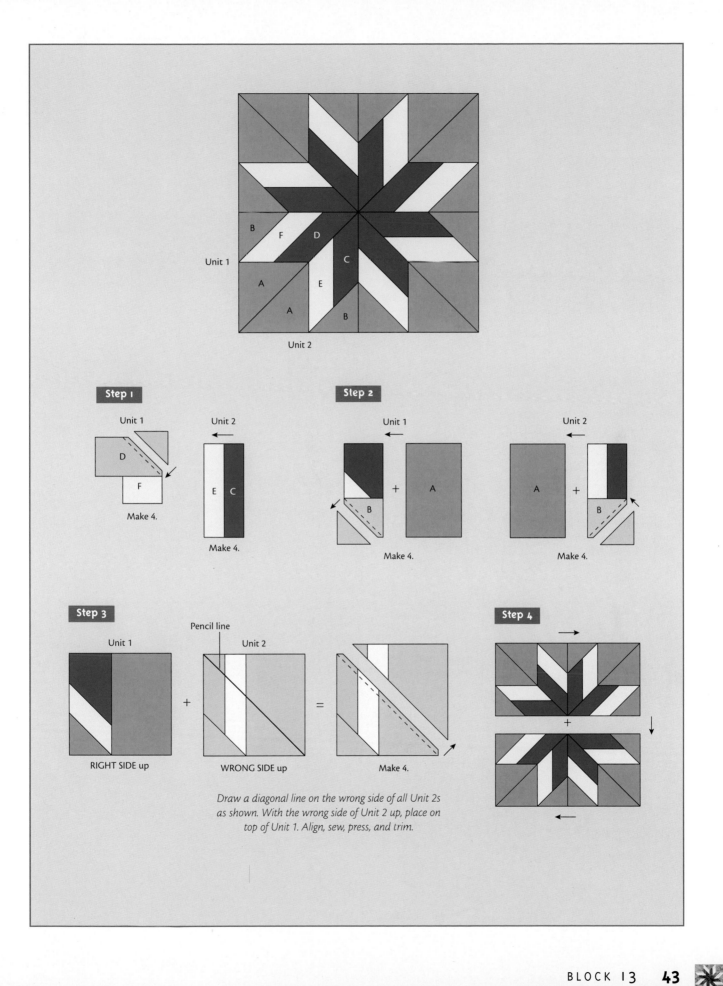

Unit 1

B · F · D · C

A · E

A · B

Unit 2

Step 1

Unit 1

D · F

Make 4.

Unit 2

E · C

Make 4.

Step 2

Unit 1

+ B · A

Make 4.

Unit 2

A + B

Make 4.

Step 3

Unit 1

Pencil line

Unit 2

+ = Make 4.

RIGHT SIDE up

WRONG SIDE up

Draw a diagonal line on the wrong side of all Unit 2s as shown. With the wrong side of Unit 2 up, place on top of Unit 1. Align, sew, press, and trim.

Step 4

+

Block 14

			BLOCK SIZE				
USED FOR	COLOR	NUMBER TO CUT	6"	8"	9"	10"	11"
A		8	2¼ x 3½	2⅞ x 4½	3⅛ x 5	3½ x 5½	3¾ x 6
B		8	1¾	2⅛	2⅜	2½	2¾
C		8	1½ x 2⅞	1¾ x 3⅝	2 x 4⅛	2⅛ x 4⅝	2⅜ x 5⅛
D		8	1½ x 2⅛	1¾ x 2⅝	2 x 2⅞	2⅛ x 3	2⅜ x 3¼
E		8	¾ x 3½	⅞ x 4½	⅞ x 5	⅞ x 5½	⅞ x 6

			12"	14"	15"	16"	18"
A		8	4 x 6½	4⅝ x 7½	4⅞ x 8	5¼ x 8½	5¾ x 9½
B		8	3	3⅜	3⅝	3¾	4¼
C		8	2½ x 5¼	2⅞ x 6¼	3 x 6½	3⅛ x 7	3½ x 7⅝
D		8	2½ x 3¾	2⅞ x 4⅛	3 x 4½	3⅛ x 4⅝	3½ x 5⅜
E		8	1 x 6½	1 x 7½	1⅛ x 8	1⅛ x 8½	1¼ x 9½

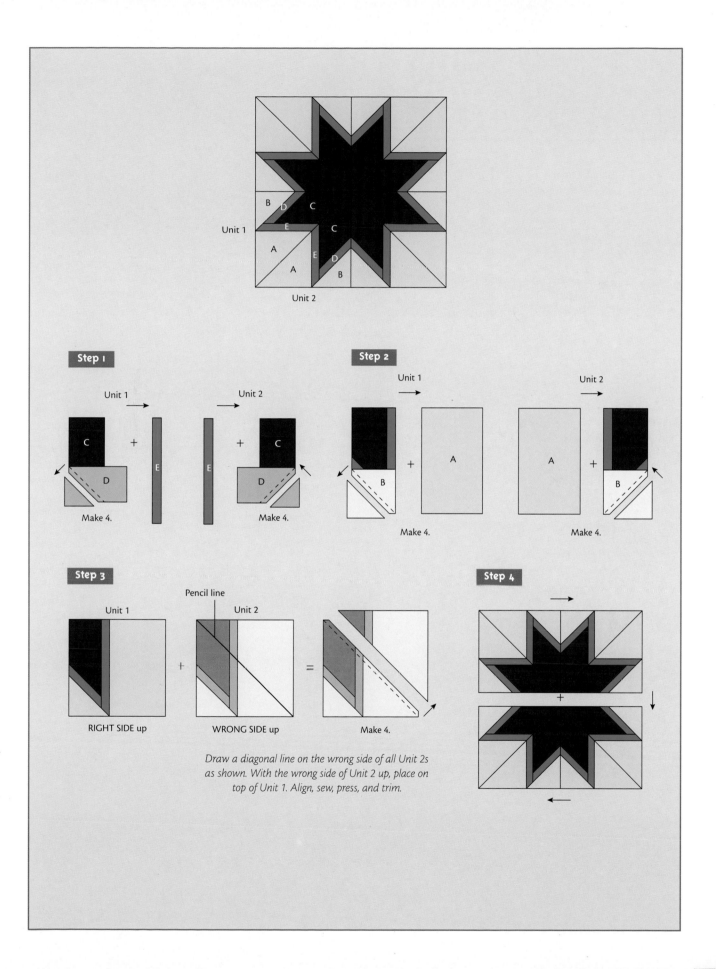

Unit 1

Unit 2

Step 1

Unit 1 →

C

D

E

+

Make 4.

E

+

D

C

Unit 2 ←

Make 4.

Step 2

Unit 1 →

C

B

+

A

Make 4.

A

+

C

B

Unit 2 →

Make 4.

Step 3

Unit 1

Pencil line

Unit 2

RIGHT SIDE up

+

WRONG SIDE up

=

Make 4.

Draw a diagonal line on the wrong side of all Unit 2s as shown. With the wrong side of Unit 2 up, place on top of Unit 1. Align, sew, press, and trim.

Step 4

+

Block 15

USED FOR	COLOR	NUMBER TO CUT	BLOCK SIZE				
			4"	6"	8"	9"	10"
A		8	1⅝ x 2½	2¼ x 3½	2⅞ x 4½	3⅛ x 5	3½ x 5½
B		8	1⅜	1¾	2⅛	2⅜	2½
C		8	1⅜ x 2½	1¾ x 3½	2⅛ x 4½	2⅜ x 5	2½ x 5½
D		8	1⅜	1¾	2⅛	2⅜	2½

USED FOR	COLOR	NUMBER TO CUT	12"	14"	15"	16"	18"
A		8	4 x 6½	4⅝ x 7½	4⅞ x 8	5¼ x 8½	5¾ x 9½
B		8	3	3⅜	3⅝	3¾	4¼
C		8	3 x 6½	3⅜ x 7½	3⅝ x 8	3¾ x 8½	4¼ x 9½
D		8	3	3⅜	3⅝	3¾	4¼

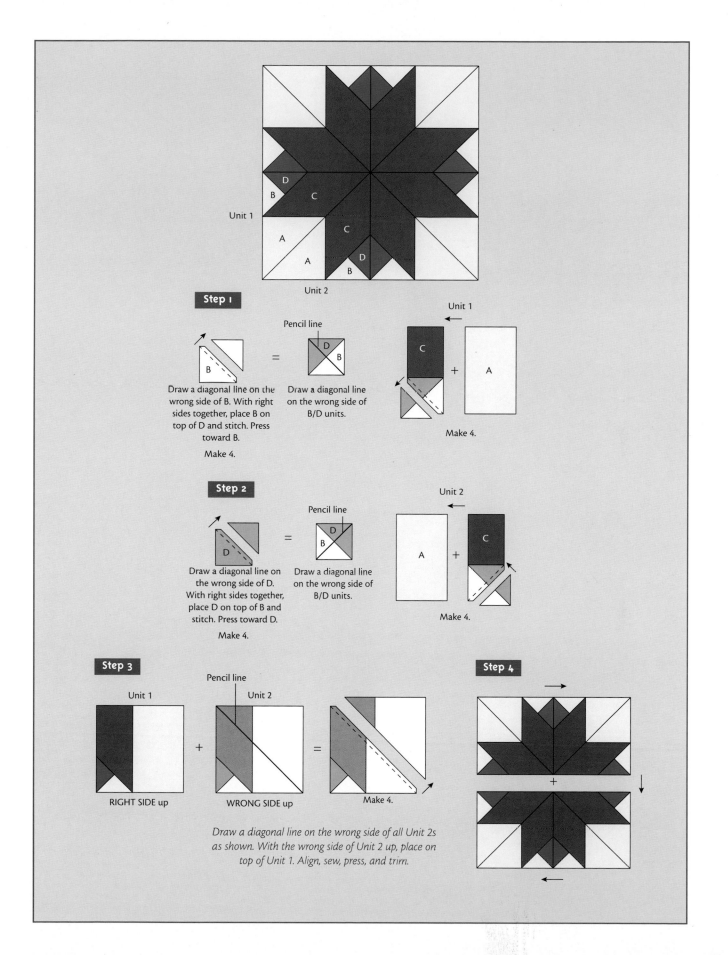

Step 1

Draw a diagonal line on the wrong side of B. With right sides together, place B on top of D and stitch. Press toward B.

Make 4.

Pencil line

Draw a diagonal line on the wrong side of B/D units.

Unit 1

C + A

Make 4.

Step 2

Draw a diagonal line on the wrong side of D. With right sides together, place D on top of B and stitch. Press toward D.

Make 4.

Pencil line

Draw a diagonal line on the wrong side of B/D units.

Unit 2

A + C

Make 4.

Step 3

Unit 1   Pencil line   Unit 2

RIGHT SIDE up   +   WRONG SIDE up   =   Make 4.

Draw a diagonal line on the wrong side of all Unit 2s as shown. With the wrong side of Unit 2 up, place on top of Unit 1. Align, sew, press, and trim.

Step 4

<table>
BLOCK SIZE
</table>

USED FOR	COLOR	NUMBER TO CUT	6"	8"	9"	10"	11"
A		8	2¼ x 3½	2⅞ x 4½	3⅛ x 5	3½ x 5½	3¾ x 6
B		8	1¾	2⅛	2⅜	2½	2¾
C		4	1¾ x 2¾	2⅛ x 3½	2⅜ x 3⅞	2½ x 4¼	2¾ x 4⅝
D		4	1¾ x 2	2⅛ x 2½	2⅜ x 2¾	2½ x 3	2¾ x 3¼
E		8	1¼ x 1¾	1½ x 2⅛	1⅝ x 2⅜	1¾ x 2½	1⅞ x 2¾
F		4	1¼ x 1¾	1½ x 2⅛	1⅝ x 2⅜	1¾ x 2½	1⅞ x 2¾

USED FOR	COLOR	NUMBER TO CUT	12"	14"	15"	16"	18"
A		8	4 x 6½	4⅝ x 7½	4⅞ x 8	5¼ x 8½	5¾ x 9½
B		8	3	3⅜	3⅝	3¾	4¼
C		4	3 x 5	3⅜ x 5¾	3⅝ x 6⅛	3¾ x 6½	4¼ x 7¼
D		4	3 x 3½	3⅜ x 4	3⅝ x 4¼	3¾ x 4½	4¼ x 5
E		8	2 x 3	2¼ x 3⅜	2⅜ x 3⅝	2½ x 3¾	2¾ x 4¼
F		4	2 x 3	2¼ x 3⅜	2⅜ x 3⅝	2½ x 3¾	2¾ x 4¼

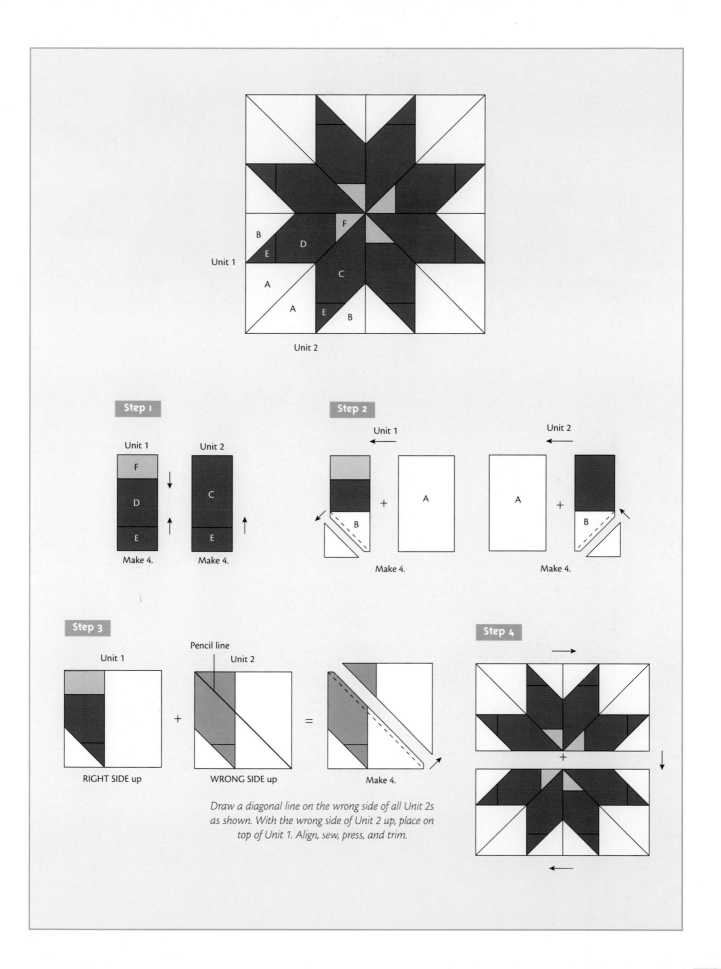

Unit 1

Unit 2

Step 1

Unit 1 — F, D, E
Make 4.

Unit 2 — C, E
Make 4.

Step 2

Unit 1

B
+ A
Make 4.

Unit 2

A +
B
Make 4.

Step 3

Unit 1
RIGHT SIDE up

Pencil line
Unit 2
WRONG SIDE up

=
Make 4.

Draw a diagonal line on the wrong side of all Unit 2s as shown. With the wrong side of Unit 2 up, place on top of Unit 1. Align, sew, press, and trim.

Step 4

+

Block 17

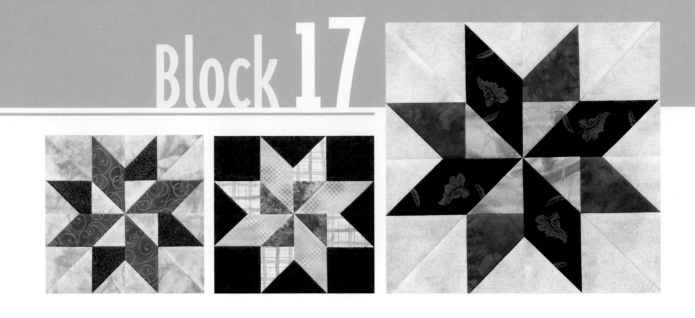

				BLOCK SIZE			
USED FOR	COLOR	NUMBER TO CUT	6"	8"	9"	10"	11"
A		8	2¼ x 3½	2⅞ x 4½	3⅛ x 5	3½ x 5½	3¾ x 6
B		8	1¾	2⅛	2⅜	2½	2¾
C		4	1¾ x 3½	2⅛ x 4½	2⅜ x 5	2½ x 5½	2¾ x 6
D		4	1¾ x 2¼	2⅛ x 2⅞	2⅜ x 3⅛	2½ x 3½	2¾ x 3¾
E		4	1¾	2⅛	2⅜	2½	2¾

			12"	14"	15"	16"	18"
A		8	4 x 6½	4⅝ x 7½	4⅞ x 8	5¼ x 8½	5¾ x 9½
B		8	3	3⅜	3⅝	3¾	4¼
C		4	3 x 6½	3⅜ x 7½	3⅝ x 8	3¾ x 8½	4¼ x 9½
D		4	3 x 4	3⅜ x 4⅝	3⅝ x 4⅞	3¾ x 5¼	4¼ x 5¾
E		4	3	3⅜	3⅝	3¾	4¼

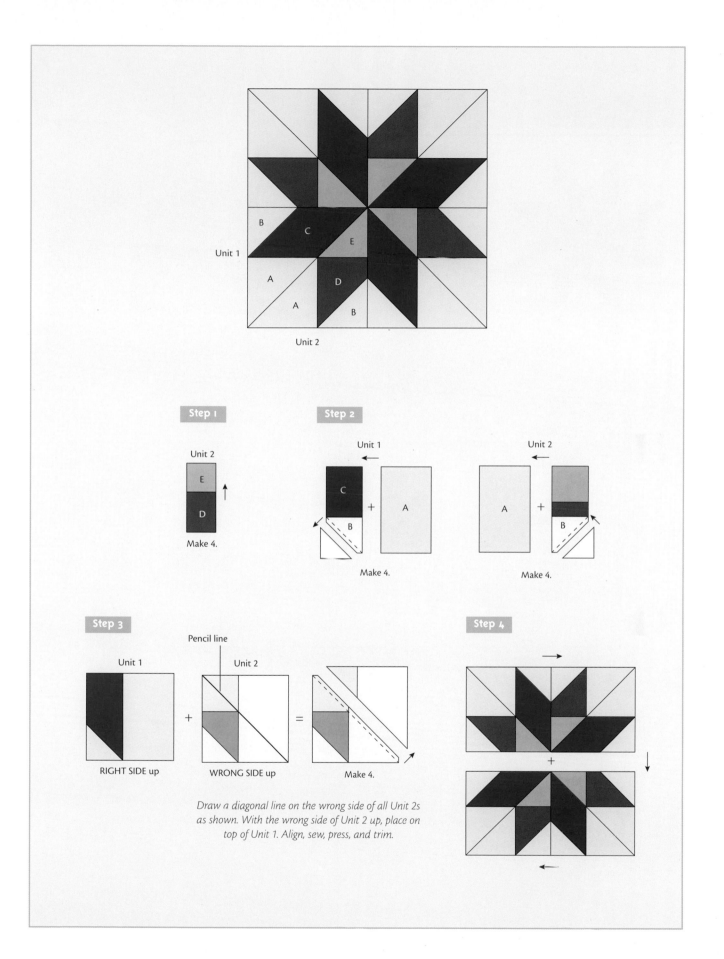

Step 1

Unit 2

E

D

Make 4.

Step 2

Unit 1

C

B

+

A

Make 4.

Unit 2

A

+

B

Make 4.

Step 3

Pencil line

Unit 1

+

Unit 2

=

Make 4.

RIGHT SIDE up

WRONG SIDE up

Draw a diagonal line on the wrong side of all Unit 2s as shown. With the wrong side of Unit 2 up, place on top of Unit 1. Align, sew, press, and trim.

Step 4

+

Block 18

BLOCK SIZE

USED FOR	COLOR	NUMBER TO CUT	6"	10"	11"	12"
A		8	2¼ x 3½	3½ x 5½	3¾ x 6	4 x 6½
B		8	1¾	2½	2¾	3
C		4	1⅛ x 3½	1½ x 5½	1⅝ x 6	1¾ x 6½
D		4	1¾ x 2⅝	2½ x 4	2¾ x 4⅜	3 x 4¾
E		4	1⅛ x 2	1½ x 3	1⅝ x 3¼	1¾ x 3½
F		4	1⅛ x 2⅝	1½ x 4	1⅝ x 4⅜	1¾ x 4¾
G		8	1⅛ x 2⅝	1½ x 4	1⅝ x 4⅜	1¾ x 4¾

			16"	17"	18"
A		8	5¼ x 8½	5½ x 9	5¾ x 9½
B		8	3¾	4	4¼
C		4	2⅛ x 8½	2¼ x 9	2⅜ x 9½
D		4	3¾ x 6⅛	4 x 6½	4¼ x 6⅞
E		4	2⅛ x 4½	2¼ x 4¾	2⅜ x 5
F		4	2⅛ x 6⅛	2¼ x 6½	2⅜ x 6⅞
G		8	2⅛ x 6⅛	2¼ x 6½	2⅜ x 6⅞

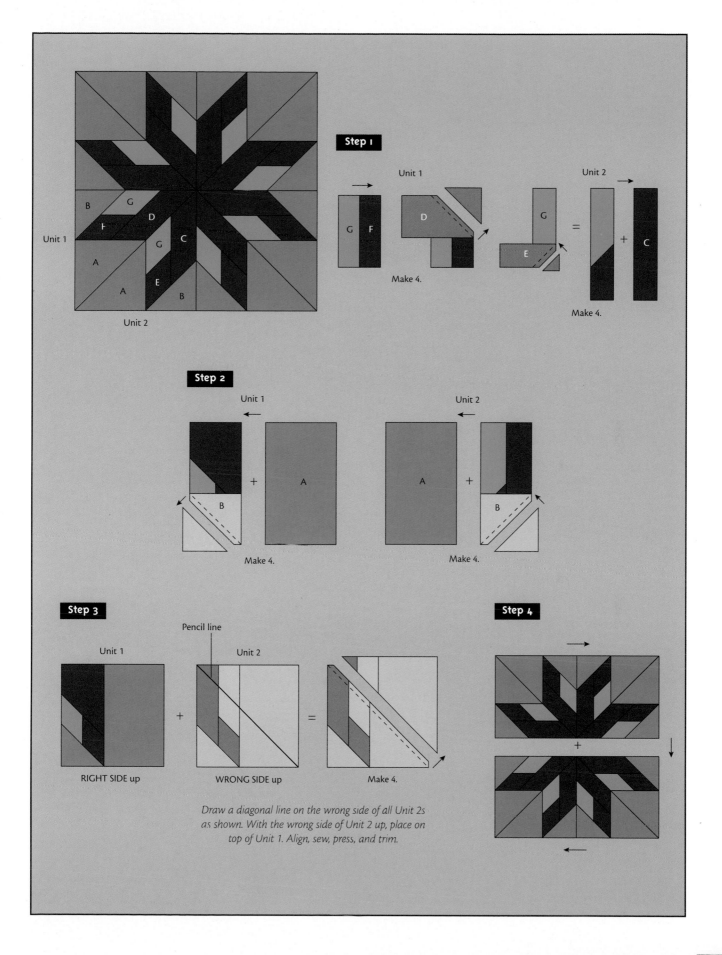

Step 1

Unit 1

Make 4.

Unit 2

Make 4.

Step 2

Unit 1

+ A

Make 4.

Unit 2

A +

Make 4.

Step 3

Pencil line

Unit 1

RIGHT SIDE up

+

Unit 2

WRONG SIDE up

=

Make 4.

Draw a diagonal line on the wrong side of all Unit 2s as shown. With the wrong side of Unit 2 up, place on top of Unit 1. Align, sew, press, and trim.

Step 4

+

Block 19

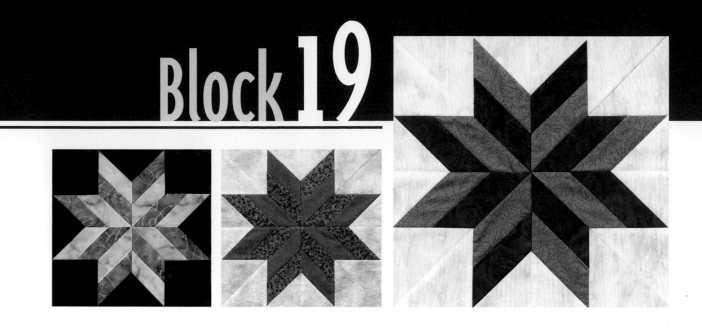

USED FOR	COLOR	NUMBER TO CUT	6"	10"	11"	12"
A		8	2¼ x 3½	3½ x 5½	3¾ x 6	4 x 6½
B		8	1¾	2½	2¾	3
C		8	1¾ x 2⅝	2½ x 4	2¾ x 4⅜	3 x 4¾
D		8	1¾ x 2⅝	2½ x 4	2¾ x 4⅜	3 x 4¾

USED FOR	COLOR	NUMBER TO CUT	16"	17"	18"
A		8	5¼ x 8½	5½ x 9	5¾ x 9½
B		8	3¾	4	4¼
C		8	3¾ x 6⅛	4 x 6½	4¼ x 6⅞
D		8	3¾ x 6⅛	4 x 6½	4¼ x 6⅞

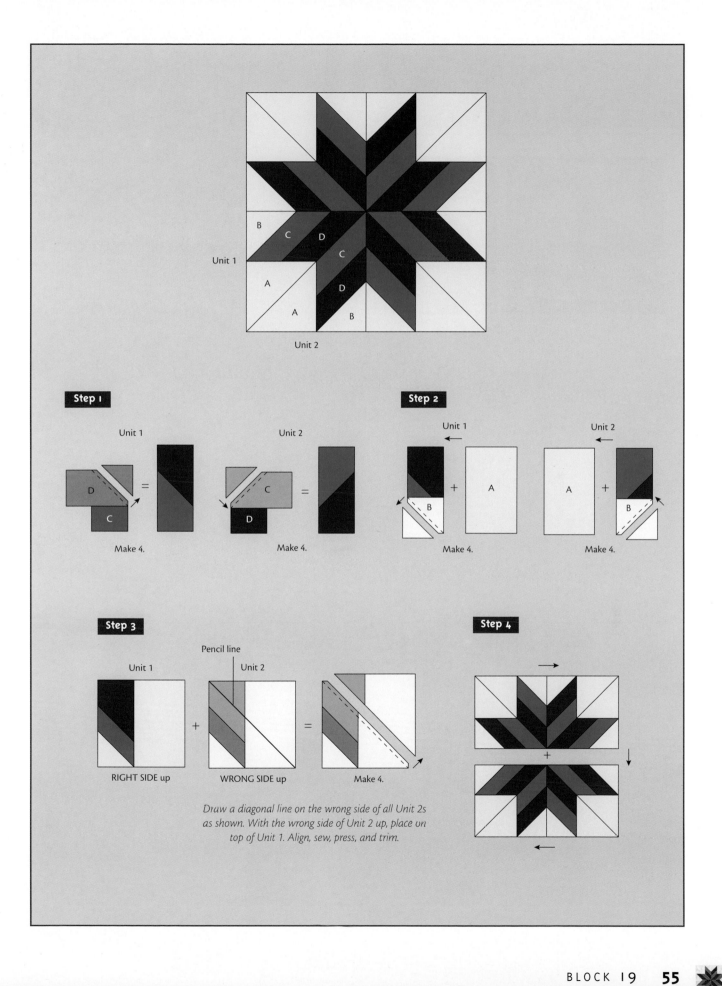

Unit 1

Unit 2

Step 1

Unit 1

= Make 4.

Unit 2

= Make 4.

Step 2

Unit 1

+ Make 4.

Unit 2

+ Make 4.

Step 3

Pencil line

Unit 1   Unit 2

+   =   Make 4.

RIGHT SIDE up   WRONG SIDE up

Draw a diagonal line on the wrong side of all Unit 2s as shown. With the wrong side of Unit 2 up, place on top of Unit 1. Align, sew, press, and trim.

Step 4

+

Block 20

USED FOR	COLOR	NUMBER TO CUT	BLOCK SIZE			
			6"	10"	11"	12"
A		8	2¼ x 3½	3½ x 5½	3¾ x 6	4 x 6½
B		8	1⅛ x 2	1½ x 3	1⅝ x 3¼	1¾ x 3½
C		8	1⅛	1½	1⅝	1¾
D		8	1⅛ x 2⅞	1½ x 4½	1⅝ x 4⅞	1¾ x 5¼
E		8	1⅛ x 1¾	1½ x 2½	1⅝ x 2¾	1¾ x 3
F		8	1⅛ x 2⅝	1½ x 4	1⅝ x 4⅜	1¾ x 4¾

USED FOR	COLOR	NUMBER TO CUT	16"	17"	18"
A		8	5¼ x 8½	5½ x 9	5¾ x 9½
B		8	2⅛ x 4½	2¼ x 4¾	2⅜ x 5
C		8	2⅛	2¼	2⅜
D		8	2⅛ x 6⅞	2¼ x 7¼	2⅜ x 7⅝
E		8	2⅛ x 3¾	2¼ x 4	2⅜ x 4¼
F		8	2⅛ x 6⅛	2¼ x 6½	2⅜ x 6⅞

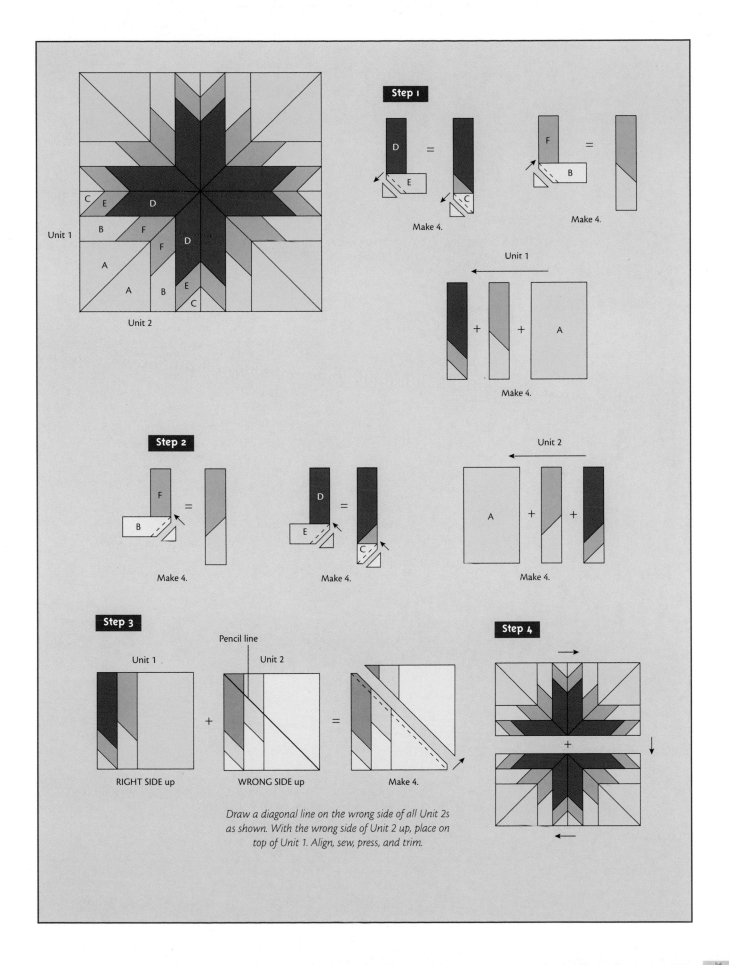

Unit 1

Unit 2

Step 1

D = E C

Make 4.

F = B

Make 4.

Unit 1

+ + A

Make 4.

Step 2

F = B

Make 4.

D = E C

Make 4.

Unit 2

A + +

Make 4.

Step 3

Unit 1

Pencil line

Unit 2

+ =

RIGHT SIDE up   WRONG SIDE up   Make 4.

Draw a diagonal line on the wrong side of all Unit 2s as shown. With the wrong side of Unit 2 up, place on top of Unit 1. Align, sew, press, and trim.

Step 4

+

Block 21

USED FOR	COLOR	NUMBER TO CUT	BLOCK SIZE			
			6"	10"	11"	12"
A		8	2¼ x 2⅞	3½ x 4½	3¾ x 4⅞	4 x 5¼
B		8	1¾	2½	2¾	3
C		8	1⅛ x 1⅜	1½ x 2	1⅝ x 2⅛	1¾ x 2¼
D		16	1⅛ x 2	1½ x 3	1⅝ x 3¼	1¾ x 3½
E		16	1⅛ x 2⅝	1½ x 4	1⅝ x 4⅜	1¾ x 4¾
F		8	1⅛ x 2	1½ x 3	1⅝ x 3¼	1¾ x 3½

USED FOR	COLOR	NUMBER TO CUT	16"	17"	18"
A		8	5¼ x 6⅞	5½ x 7¼	5¾ x 7⅝
B		8	3¾	4	4¼
C		8	2⅛ x 2⅞	2¼ x 3	2⅜ x 3⅛
D		16	2⅛ x 4½	2¼ x 4¾	2⅜ x 5
E		16	2⅛ x 6⅛	2¼ x 6½	2⅜ x 6⅞
F		8	2⅛ x 4½	2¼ x 4¾	2⅜ x 5

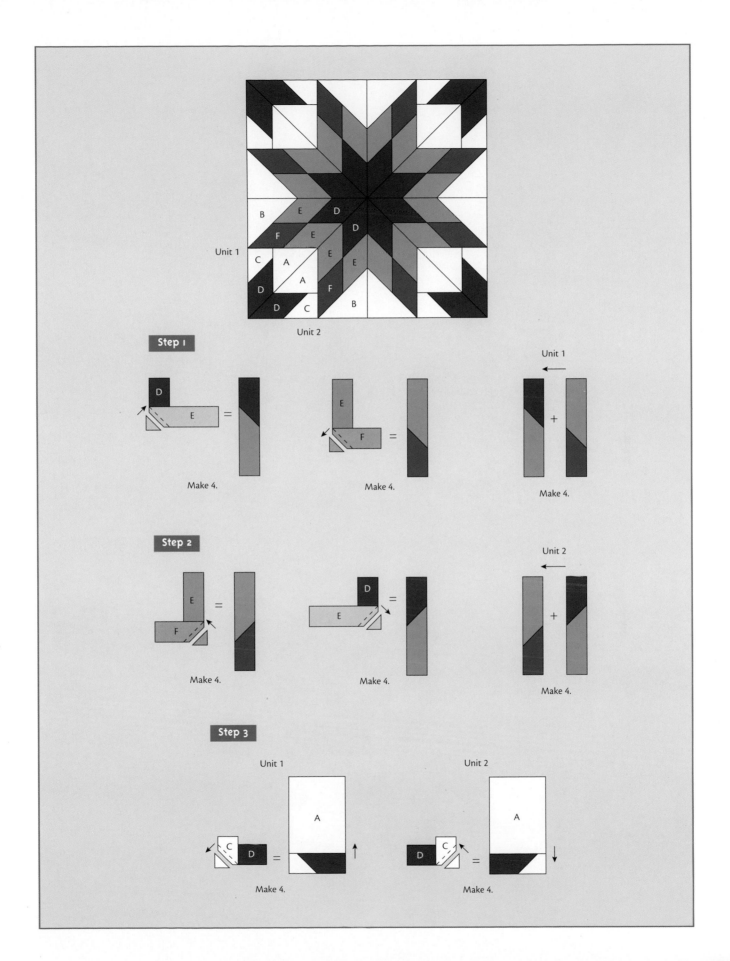

Unit 1

Unit 2

Step 1

Make 4.

Make 4.

Unit 1

Make 4.

Step 2

Make 4.

Make 4.

Unit 2

Make 4.

Step 3

Unit 1

Unit 2

Make 4.

Make 4.

Step 4

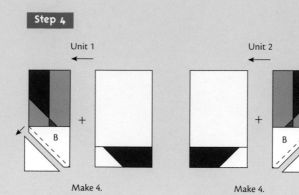

Unit 1   Unit 2

B   +   +   B

Make 4.   Make 4.

Step 5

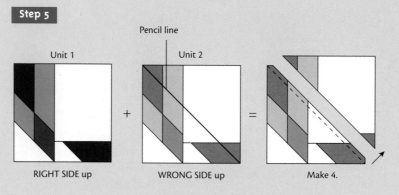

Pencil line

Unit 1   Unit 2

+   =   Make 4.

RIGHT SIDE up   WRONG SIDE up

*Draw a diagonal line on the wrong side of all Unit 2s
as shown. With the wrong side of Unit 2 up, place on
top of Unit 1. Align, sew, press, and trim.*

Step 6

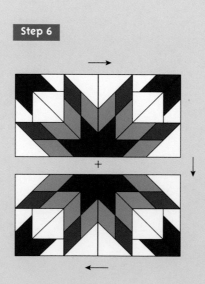

+

Block 22

BLOCK SIZE

USED FOR	COLOR	NUMBER TO CUT	6"	10"	11"	12"
A		8	1⅝ x 3½	2½ x 5½	2⅝ x 6	2¾ x 6½
B		8	1¾	2½	2¾	3
C		8	1⅛ x 1⅜	1½ x 2	1⅝ x 2⅛	1¾ x 2¼
D		8	1⅛ x 2	1½ x 3	1⅝ x 3¼	1¾ x 3½
E		16	1⅛ x 2⅝	1½ x 4	1⅝ x 4⅜	1¾ x 4¾
F		8	1⅛ x 2	1½ x 3	1⅝ x 3¼	1¾ x 3½
G		8	1⅛ x 3¼	1½ x 5	1⅝ x 5½	1¾ x 6

USED FOR	COLOR	NUMBER TO CUT	16"	17"	18"
A		8	3⅝ x 8½	3¾ x 9	3⅞ x 9½
B		8	3¾	4	4¼
C		8	2⅛ x 2⅞	2¼ x 3	2⅜ x 3⅛
D		8	2⅛ x 4½	2¼ x 4¾	2⅜ x 5
E		16	2⅛ x 6⅛	2¼ x 6½	2⅜ x 6⅞
F		8	2⅛ x 4½	2¼ x 4¾	2⅜ x 5
G		8	2⅛ x 7¾	2¼ x 8¼	2⅜ x 8¾

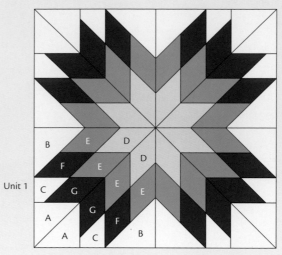

Unit 1

Unit 2

Step 1

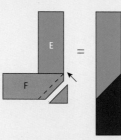

Make 4.

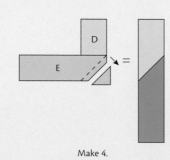

Make 4.

Unit 1

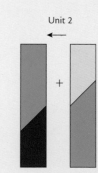

Make 4.

Step 2

Make 4.

Make 4.

Unit 2

Make 4.

Step 3

Unit 1   Unit 2

G   G

C   C

Make 4.   Make 4.

Step 4

Unit 1

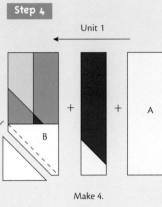

+   B   +   A

Make 4.

Unit 2

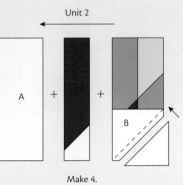

A   +   +   B

Make 4.

Step 5

Pencil line

Unit 1   Unit 2

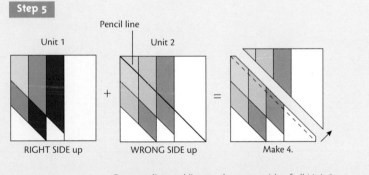

+   =

RIGHT SIDE up   WRONG SIDE up   Make 4.

Draw a diagonal line on the wrong side of all Unit 2s as shown. With the wrong side of Unit 2 up, place on top of Unit 1. Align, sew, press, and trim.

Step 6

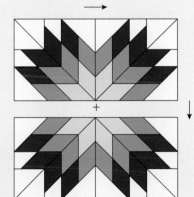

+

Block 23

USED FOR	COLOR	NUMBER TO CUT	**BLOCK SIZE**				
			4"	6"	8"	9"	10"
A		6	1⅝ x 2½	2¼ x 3½	2⅞ x 4½	3⅛ x 5	3½ x 5½
B		6	1⅜	1¾	2⅛	2⅜	2½
C		2	2¼	3⅛	4	4½	4⅞
D		6	1⅜ x 2½	1¾ x 3½	2⅛ x 4½	2⅜ x 5	2½ x 5½
E		1	2½	3½	4½	5	5½
F		1	1½	2⅛	2⅝	3	3¼

USED FOR	COLOR	NUMBER TO CUT	12"	14"	15"	16"	18"
A		6	4 x 6½	4⅝ x 7½	4⅞ x 8	5¼ x 8½	5¾ x 9½
B		6	3	3⅜	3⅝	3¾	4¼
C		2	5¾	6⅝	7	7½	8⅜
D		6	3 x 6½	3⅜ x 7½	3⅝ x 8	3¾ x 8½	4¼ x 9½
E		1	6½	7½	8	8½	9½
F		1	3¾	4¼	4½	4⅞	5⅜

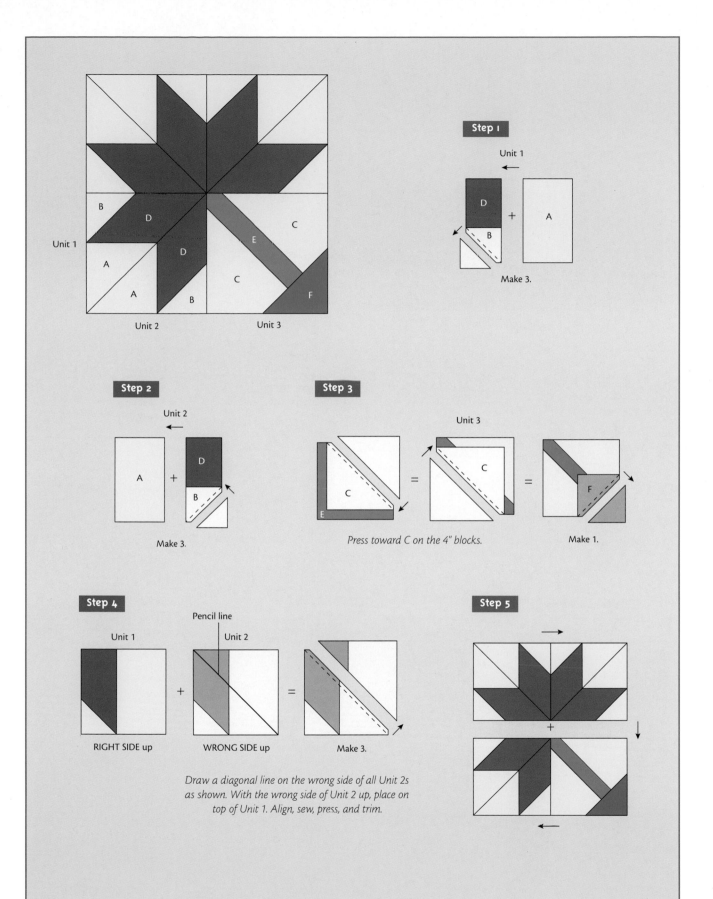

Step 1

Unit 1

D
B + A

Make 3.

Step 2

Unit 2

A + D
B

Make 3.

Step 3

Unit 3

C
E = C = F

Press toward C on the 4" blocks.

Make 1.

Step 4

Pencil line

Unit 1   Unit 2

+ = Make 3.

RIGHT SIDE up   WRONG SIDE up

*Draw a diagonal line on the wrong side of all Unit 2s
as shown. With the wrong side of Unit 2 up, place on
top of Unit 1. Align, sew, press, and trim.*

Step 5

+

Block 24

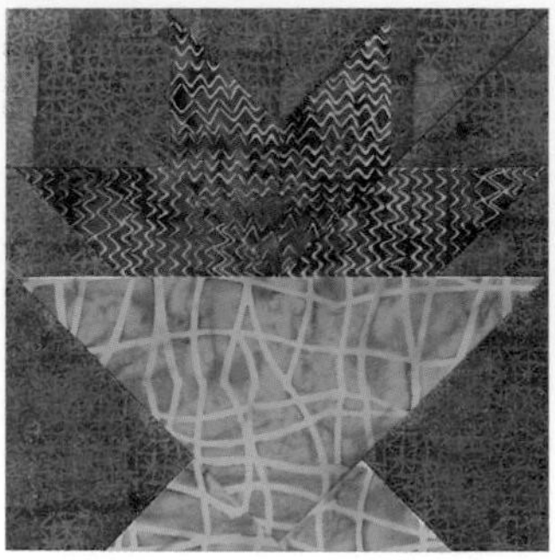

USED FOR	COLOR	NUMBER TO CUT	**BLOCK SIZE**				
			4"	6"	8"	9"	10"
A		4	1⅝ x 2½	2¼ x 3½	2⅞ x 4½	3⅛ x 5	3½ x 5½
B		4	1⅜	1¾	2⅛	2⅜	2½
C		2	2½	3½	4½	5	5½
D		4	1⅜ x 2½	1¾ x 3½	2⅛ x 4½	2⅜ x 5	2½ x 5½
E		1	2½ x 4½	3½ x 6½	4½ x 8½	5 x 9½	5½ x 10½
F		2	1¾	2⅜	3	3⅜	3⅝

USED FOR	COLOR	NUMBER TO CUT	12"	14"	15"	16"	18"
A		4	4 x 6½	4⅝ x 7½	4⅞ x 8	5¼ x 8½	5¾ x 9½
B		4	3	3⅜	3⅝	3¾	4¼
C		2	6½	7½	8	8½	9½
D		4	3 x 6½	3⅜ x 7½	3⅝ x 8	3¾ x 8½	4¼ x 9½
E		1	6½ x 12½	7½ x 14½	8 x 15½	8½ x 16½	9½ x 18½
F		2	4¼	4⅞	5¼	5½	6⅛

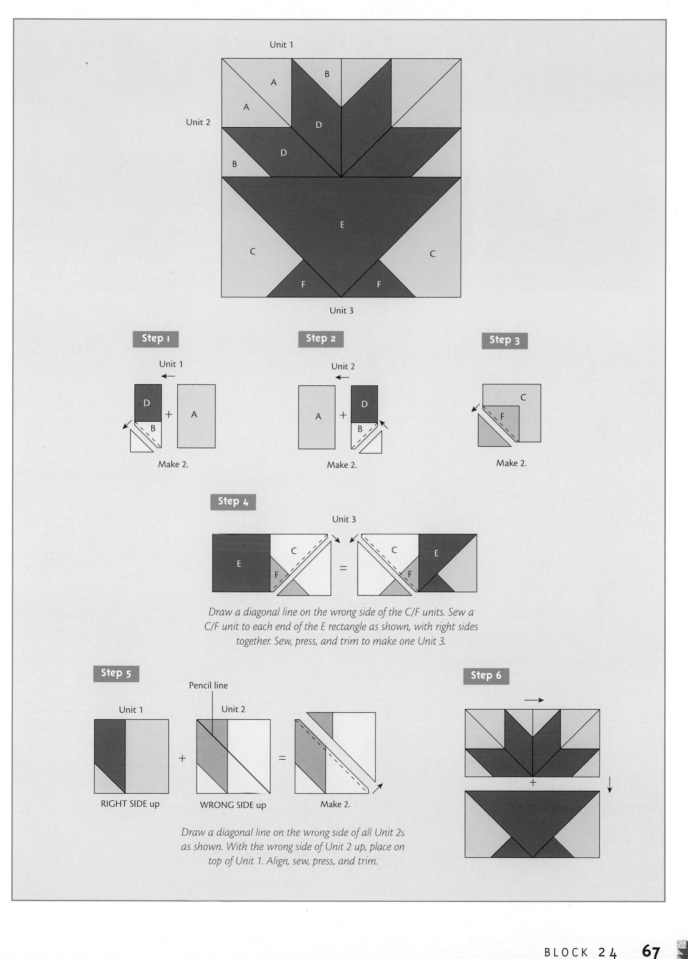

Unit 1

A B A

Unit 2

D D B

E C C F F

Unit 3

Step 1

Unit 1

D B + A

Make 2.

Step 2

Unit 2

A + D B

Make 2.

Step 3

C F

Make 2.

Step 4

Unit 3

E C F = C F E

Draw a diagonal line on the wrong side of the C/F units. Sew a C/F unit to each end of the E rectangle as shown, with right sides together. Sew, press, and trim to make one Unit 3.

Step 5

Pencil line

Unit 1 + Unit 2 =

RIGHT SIDE up   WRONG SIDE up   Make 2.

Draw a diagonal line on the wrong side of all Unit 2s as shown. With the wrong side of Unit 2 up, place on top of Unit 1. Align, sew, press, and trim.

Step 6

Block 25

			BLOCK SIZE			
USED FOR	COLOR	NUMBER TO CUT	6"	10"	11"	12"
A		4	2¼ x 3½	3½ x 5½	3¾ x 6	4 x 6½
B		4	1¾	2½	2¾	3
C		2	1¾ x 3	2½ x 4½	2¾ x 5	3 x 5½
D		2	2¼ x 3	3½ x 4½	3¾ x 5	4 x 5½
E		4	1⅛ x 2	1½ x 3	1⅝ x 3¼	1¾ x 3½
F		8	1⅛ x 2⅝	1½ x 4	1⅝ x 4⅜	1¾ x 4¾
G		4	1⅛ x 2	1½ x 3	1⅝ x 3¼	1¾ x 3½
H		1	1¾ x 4	2½ x 6½	2¾ x 7	3 x 7½
I		1	2¼ x 5	3½ x 8½	3¾ x 9	4 x 9½

			16"	17"	18"
A		4	5¼ x 8½	5½ x 9	5¾ x 9½
B		4	3¾	4	4¼
C		2	3¾ x 7	4 x 7½	4¼ x 8
D		2	5¼ x 7	5½ x 7½	5¾ x 8
E		4	2⅛ x 4½	2¼ x 4¾	2⅜ x 5
F		8	2⅛ x 6⅛	2¼ x 6½	2⅜ x 6⅞
G		4	2⅛ x 4½	2¼ x 4¾	2⅜ x 5
H		1	3¾ x 10	4 x 10½	4¼ x 11
I		1	5¼ x 13	5½ x 13½	5¾ x 14

Unit 1

Unit 2

Unit 3

Unit 4

A A G B F F G F E F E B C H C D I D

Step 1

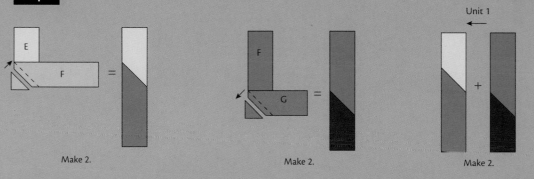

E F =

Make 2.

F G =

Make 2.

Unit 1

+

Make 2.

Step 2

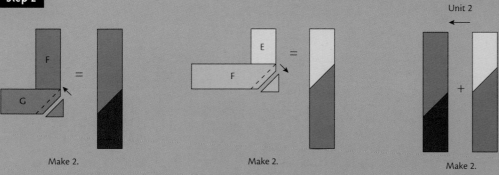

F G =

Make 2.

E F =

Make 2.

Unit 2

+

Make 2.

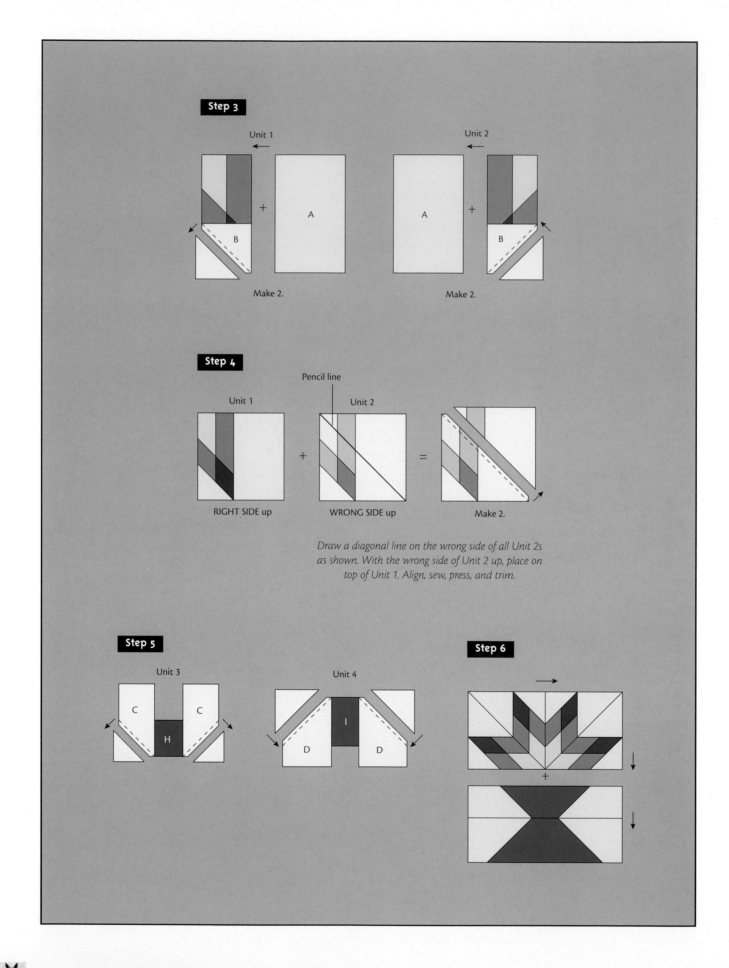

Step 3

Unit 1

Unit 2

A

+

B

Make 2.

A

+

B

Make 2.

Step 4

Pencil line

Unit 1

Unit 2

RIGHT SIDE up

+

WRONG SIDE up

=

Make 2.

Draw a diagonal line on the wrong side of all Unit 2s as shown. With the wrong side of Unit 2 up, place on top of Unit 1. Align, sew, press, and trim.

Step 5

Unit 3

C   C

H

Unit 4

I

D   D

Step 6

+

Block 26

BLOCK SIZE

USED FOR	COLOR	NUMBER TO CUT	5"	6"	7"	10"	11"
A		8	2 x 2½	2¼ x 2⅞	2½ x 3¼	3½ x 4½	3¾ x 4⅞
B		8	1 x 1½	1⅛ x 1¾	1¼ x 2	1½ x 2½	1⅝ x 2¾
C		8	1½ x 3	1¾ x 3½	2 x 4	2½ x 5½	2¾ x 6
D		4	1 x 1½	1⅛ x 1¾	1¼ x 2	1½ x 2½	1⅝ x 2¾
E		4	1 x 2	1⅛ x 2¼	1¼ x 2½	1½ x 3½	1⅝ x 3¾
F		4	1 x 1½	1⅛ x 1¾	1¼ x 2	1½ x 2½	1⅝ x 2¾
G		4	1 x 2	1⅛ x 2¼	1¼ x 2½	1½ x 3½	1⅝ x 3¾

USED FOR	COLOR	NUMBER TO CUT	12"	13"	16"	17"	18"
A		8	4 x 5¼	4¼ x 5⅝	5¼ x 6⅞	5½ x 7¼	5¾ x 7⅝
B		8	1¾ x 3	1⅞ x 3¼	2⅛ x 3¾	2¼ x 4	2⅜ x 4¼
C		8	3 x 6½	3¼ x 7	3¾ x 8½	4 x 9	4¼ x 9½
D		4	1¾ x 3	1⅞ x 3¼	2⅛ x 3¾	2¼ x 4	2⅜ x 4¼
E		4	1¾ x 4	1⅞ x 4¼	2⅛ x 5¼	2¼ x 5½	2⅜ x 5¾
F		4	1¾ x 3	1⅞ x 3¼	2⅛ x 3¾	2¼ x 4	2⅜ x 4¼
G		4	1¾ x 4	1⅞ x 4¼	2⅛ x 5¼	2¼ x 5½	2⅜ x 5¾

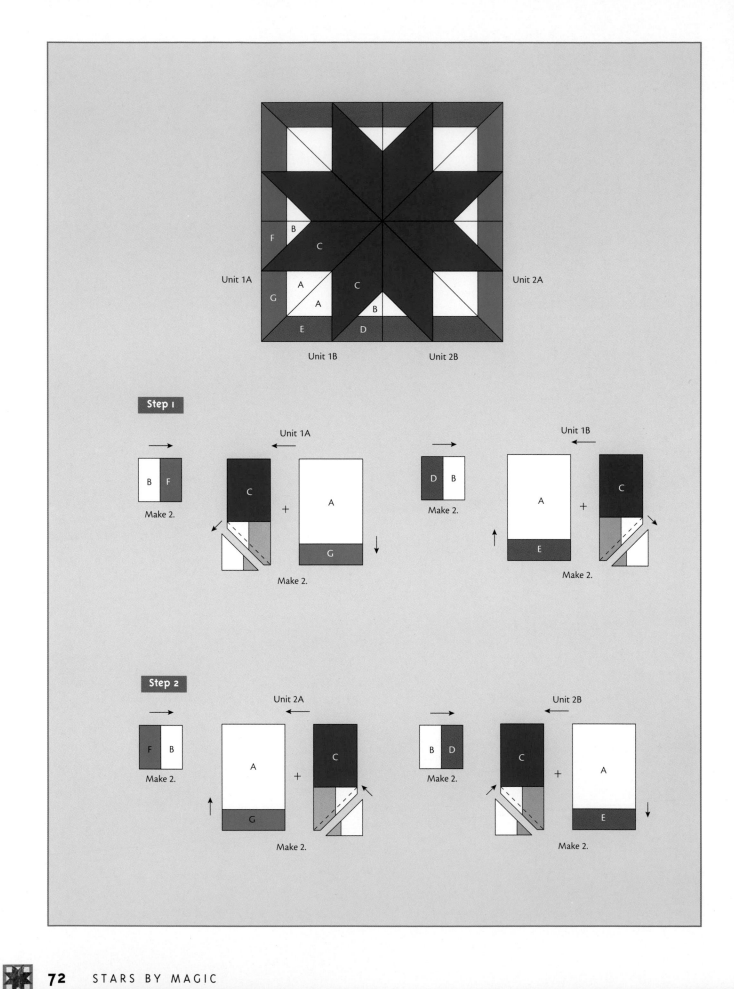

Step 1

Unit 1A

B | F

Make 2.

C + A G

Make 2.

Unit 1B

D | B

Make 2.

A E + C

Make 2.

Step 2

Unit 2A

F | B

Make 2.

A G + C

Make 2.

Unit 2B

B | D

Make 2.

C + A E

Make 2.

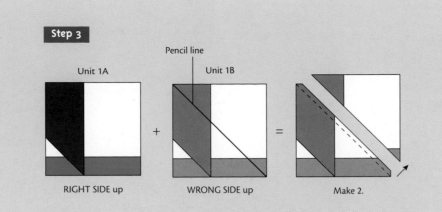

Pencil line

Unit 1A

Unit 1B

+

=

RIGHT SIDE up

WRONG SIDE up

Make 2.

Draw a diagonal line on the wrong side of the two Unit 1Bs as shown. With the wrong side of Unit 1B up, place on top of Unit 1A. Align, sew, press, and trim.

Step 4

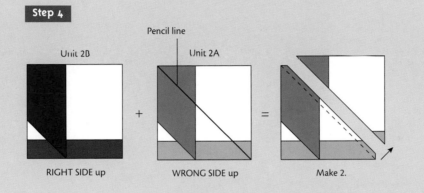

Pencil line

Unit 2B

Unit 2A

+

=

RIGHT SIDE up

WRONG SIDE up

Make 2.

Draw a diagonal line on the wrong side of the two Unit 2As as shown. With the wrong side of Unit 2A up, place on top of Unit 2B. Align, sew, press, and trim.

Step 5

Unit 2A-2B → Unit 1A-1B

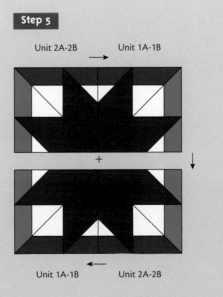

+

Unit 1A-1B ← Unit 2A-2B

Block 27

			BLOCK SIZE				
USED FOR	COLOR	NUMBER TO CUT	6"	8"	9"	10"	11"
A		8	1¼ x 3½	1½ x 4½	1⅝ x 5	1¾ x 5½	1⅞ x 6
B		8	2¾	3½	3⅞	4¼	4⅝
C		8	1¼ x 3½	1½ x 4½	1⅝ x 5	1¾ x 5½	1⅞ x 6
D		8	2 x 3½	2½ x 4½	2¾ x 5	3 x 5½	3¼ x 6

			12"	14"	15"	16"	18"
A		8	2 x 6½	2¼ x 7½	2⅜ x 8	2½ x 8½	2¾ x 9½
B		8	5	5¾	6⅛	6½	7¼
C		8	2 x 6½	2¼ x 7½	2⅜ x 8	2½ x 8½	2¾ x 9½
D		8	3½ x 6½	4 x 7½	4¼ x 8	4½ x 8½	5 x 9½

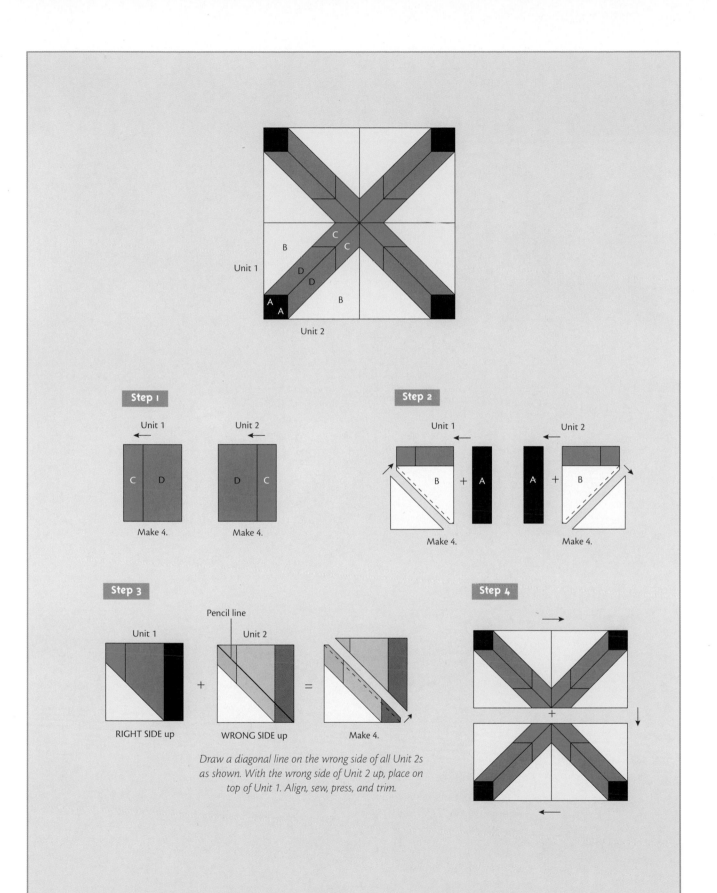

Step 1

Unit 1 ←

C D

Make 4.

Unit 2 ←

D C

Make 4.

Step 2

Unit 1 ←

B + A

Make 4.

Unit 2 ←

A + B

Make 4.

Step 3

Unit 1

C D (Pencil line)

RIGHT SIDE up

+

Unit 2 (Pencil line)

WRONG SIDE up

=

Make 4.

Draw a diagonal line on the wrong side of all Unit 2s as shown. With the wrong side of Unit 2 up, place on top of Unit 1. Align, sew, press, and trim.

Step 4

+

Block 28

			BLOCK SIZE				
USED FOR	COLOR	NUMBER TO CUT	6"	8"	9"	10"	11"
A		8	1¼ x 3½	1½ x 4½	1⅝ x 5	1¾ x 5½	1⅞ x 6
B		8	2¾	3½	3⅞	4¼	4⅝
C		8	2¾	3½	3⅞	4¼	4⅝
D		8	1¼ x 3½	1½ x 4½	1⅝ x 5	1¾ x 5½	1⅞ x 6
E		8	2 x 3½	2½ x 4½	2¾ x 5	3 x 5½	3¼ x 6

			12"	14"	15"	16"	18"
A		8	2 x 6½	2¼ x 7½	2⅜ x 8	2½ x 8½	2¾ x 9½
B		8	5	5¾	6⅛	6½	7¼
C		8	5	5¾	6⅛	6½	7¼
D		8	2 x 6½	2¼ x 7½	2⅜ x 8	2½ x 8½	2¾ x 9½
E		8	3½ x 6½	4 x 7½	4¼ x 8	4½ x 8½	5 x 9½

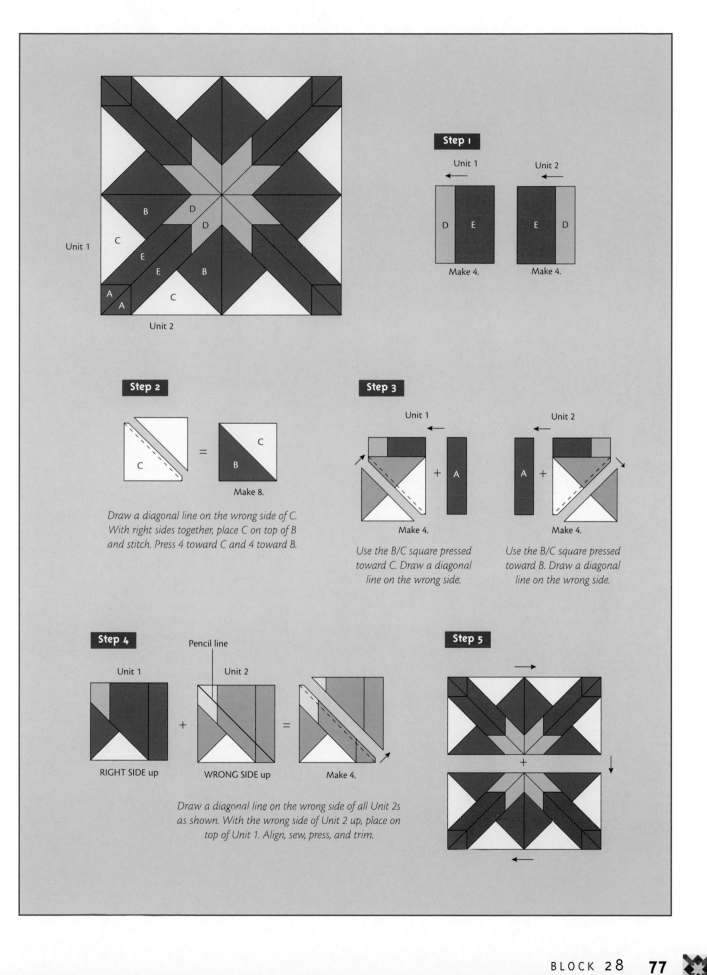

Step 1

Unit 1

Unit 2

D E

E D

Make 4.

Make 4.

Step 2

C

=

C

B

Make 8.

Draw a diagonal line on the wrong side of C. With right sides together, place C on top of B and stitch. Press 4 toward C and 4 toward B.

Step 3

Unit 1

Unit 2

+

A

A

+

Make 4.

Make 4.

Use the B/C square pressed toward C. Draw a diagonal line on the wrong side.

Use the B/C square pressed toward B. Draw a diagonal line on the wrong side.

Step 4

Pencil line

Unit 1

Unit 2

+

=

Make 4.

RIGHT SIDE up

WRONG SIDE up

Draw a diagonal line on the wrong side of all Unit 2s as shown. With the wrong side of Unit 2 up, place on top of Unit 1. Align, sew, press, and trim.

Step 5

+

Block 29

USED FOR	COLOR	NUMBER TO CUT	BLOCK SIZE				
			6"	8"	9"	10"	11"
A		8	1¼ x 3½	1½ x 4½	1⅝ x 5	1¾ x 5½	1⅞ x 6
B		8	2¾	3½	3⅞	4¼	4⅝
C		8	1¼ x 3½	1½ x 4½	1⅝ x 5	1¾ x 5½	1⅞ x 6
D		8	1¼ x 3½	1½ x 4½	1⅝ x 5	1¾ x 5½	1⅞ x 6
E		8	1¼ x 3½	1½ x 4½	1⅝ x 5	1¾ x 5½	1⅞ x 6

USED FOR	COLOR	NUMBER TO CUT	12"	14"	15"	16"	18"
A		8	2 x 6½	2¼ x 7½	2⅜ x 8	2½ x 8½	2¾ x 9½
B		8	5	5¾	6⅛	6½	7¼
C		8	2 x 6½	2¼ x 7½	2⅜ x 8	2½ x 8½	2¾ x 9½
D		8	2 x 6½	2¼ x 7½	2⅜ x 8	2½ x 8½	2¾ x 9½
E		8	2 x 6½	2¼ x 7½	2⅜ x 8	2½ x 8½	2¾ x 9½

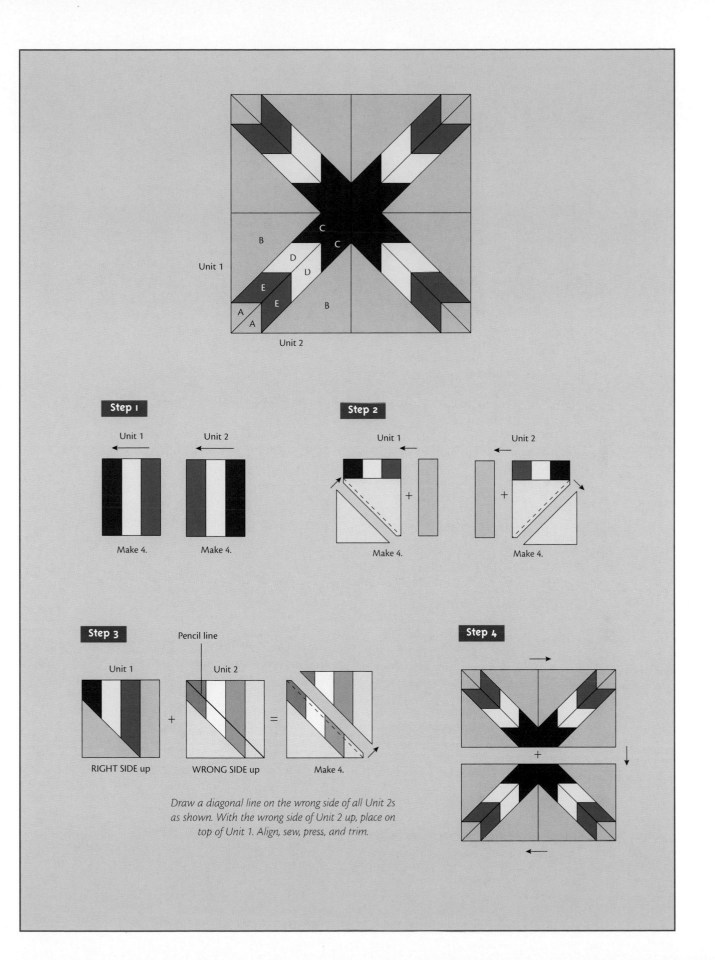

Unit 1

Unit 2

Step 1

Unit 1   Unit 2

Make 4.   Make 4.

Step 2

Unit 1   Unit 2

+   +

Make 4.   Make 4.

Step 3

Pencil line

Unit 1   Unit 2

+   =

RIGHT SIDE up   WRONG SIDE up   Make 4.

*Draw a diagonal line on the wrong side of all Unit 2s
as shown. With the wrong side of Unit 2 up, place on
top of Unit 1. Align, sew, press, and trim.*

Step 4

+

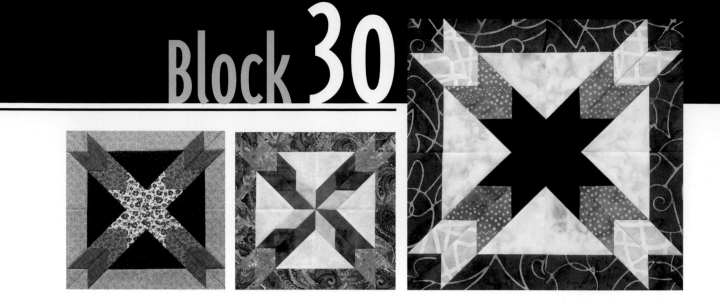

Block 30

BLOCK SIZE

USED FOR	COLOR	NUMBER TO CUT	6"	8"	9"	10"	11"
A		8	1¼ x 3½	1½ x 4½	1⅝ x 5	1¾ x 5½	1⅞ x 6
B		8	1¼ x 2¾	1½ x 3½	1⅝ x 3⅞	1¾ x 4¼	1⅞ x 4⅝
C		8	2 x 2¾	2½ x 3½	2¾ x 3⅞	3 x 4¼	3¼ x 4⅝
D		8	1¼ x 3½	1½ x 4½	1⅝ x 5	1¾ x 5½	1⅞ x 6
E		8	1¼ x 3½	1½ x 4½	1⅝ x 5	1¾ x 5½	1⅞ x 6
F		8	1¼ x 3½	1½ x 4½	1⅝ x 5	1¾ x 5½	1⅞ x 6

			12"	14"	15"	16"	18"
A		8	2 x 6½	2¼ x 7½	2⅜ x 8	2½ x 8½	2¾ x 9½
B		8	2 x 5	2¼ x 5¾	2⅜ x 6⅛	2½ x 6½	2¾ x 7¼
C		8	3½ x 5	4 x 5¾	4¼ x 6⅛	4½ x 6½	5 x 7¼
D		8	2 x 6½	2¼ x 7½	2⅜ x 8	2½ x 8½	2¾ x 9½
E		8	2 x 6½	2¼ x 7½	2⅜ x 8	2½ x 8½	2¾ x 9½
F		8	2 x 6½	2¼ x 7½	2⅜ x 8	2½ x 8½	2¾ x 9½

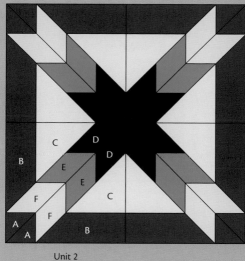

Unit 1

C D D B E E C F F A A B

Unit 2

Step 1

Unit 1 ←

Unit 2 ←

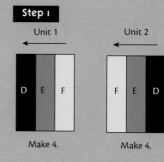

D E F
Make 4.

F E D
Make 4.

Step 2

C
B
Make 8

Press 4 toward B
and 4 toward C.

Unit 1 ←

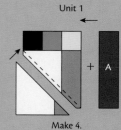 + A
Make 4.

Use the B/C square pressed
toward B. Draw a diagonal
line on the wrong side.

Unit 2 ←

A +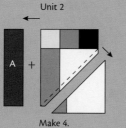
Make 4.

Use the B/C square pressed
toward C. Draw a diagonal
line on the wrong side.

Step 3

Pencil line

Unit 1   Unit 2

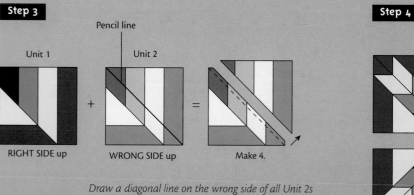

RIGHT SIDE up   WRONG SIDE up   Make 4.

Draw a diagonal line on the wrong side of all Unit 2s
as shown. With the wrong side of Unit 2 up, place on
top of Unit 1. Align, sew, press, and trim.

Step 4

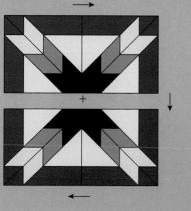

+

USING DIRECTIONAL FABRICS

Many of the blocks shown in this book include directional fabrics for the stars and the background pieces. It's fun and exciting to work with plaids and stripes for these blocks, and it's not difficult. The diagrams below will show you how easy it is to work with crosswise/lengthwise grain and directional fabric.

CUTTING AND SEWING THE BLOCKS

Visually separate the block into two sections. The two sides of the block make up the first section. For all the stripes and grain line to run lengthwise, you need to cut these four A and four C pieces on the crosswise grain of the fabric.

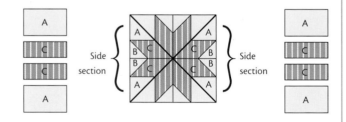

All eight of the B squares can be cut on the crosswise grain and rotated as needed. After cutting the B squares, place a little dot on the top of each square to indicate the crosswise grain.

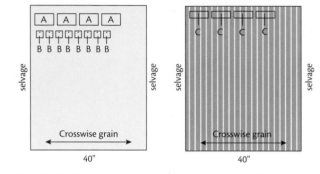

Cut all eight B squares on the crosswise grain. Put a small pencil mark at the top of each square. Cut rectangles for the two sides of the block on the crosswise grain of the fabric. Cut four A and four C pieces.

SEW MAGIC
When using directional fabrics, plan your cuts on paper before cutting your fabric, and don't cut strips the full width of the fabric. This will ensure that you won't miscut and you'll have plenty of fabric.

The second section of the block is the top and bottom. Cut these A and C pieces on the lengthwise grain of the fabric so that the stripes and grain line are correct. You do not need to cut any more B squares.

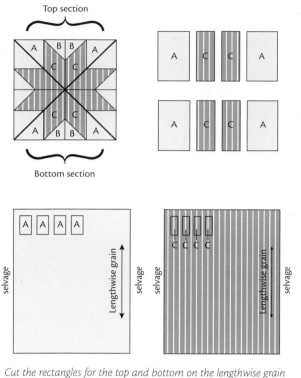

Cut the rectangles for the top and bottom on the lengthwise grain of the fabric. Cut four A and four C pieces.

When working with directional fabric, I find it's best to place the rectangle pieces on a separate cutting mat or tray to resemble the diagram below. I can then carry this to my sewing machine and sew one unit at a time. Note the position of each pencil mark on the B squares. Rotate the B pieces as shown and draw the diagonal pencil lines on the wrong side before placing them on the C rectangles. By following these directions, you will be assured the directional fabric and grain lines run correctly on your blocks.

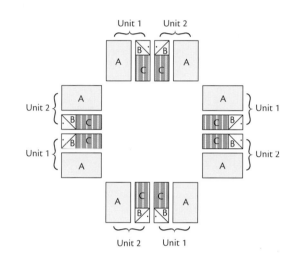

DIRECTIONAL FUN

Sometimes I want the stripes or plaids to look a certain way in the block. In those cases I cut all the star rectangles on the lengthwise grain. Other times I cut half of the pieces crosswise and half lengthwise. If you want to use a directional fabric, draw a diagram of the block you plan to make and color it to represent your fabrics. Add arrows for grainline. Then use the diagram to plan your cutting based on the direction of the pattern in your fabric and how you want it to appear in the block.

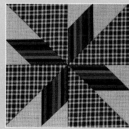

BLOCK 3 Cut all D pieces on the lengthwise grain.

BLOCK 4 Cut all C pieces on the lengthwise grain.

BLOCK 9 Cut all E pieces on the lengthwise grain.

BLOCK 10 Cut all C pieces on the lengthwise grain.

BLOCK 15 Cut half the C pieces on the crosswise grain and half on the lengthwise grain.

Those of you who know me understand that I can't stand to waste fabric. No matter how small or large, I'll find a way to use it. This personality trait came forward when I realized I would have mirror image triangle-shaped pieces left over from the Diamond-Free method. It was pretty exciting to know I would get some "bonus blocks and borders" out of what some people might call "waste." Believe it or not, there are several optional blocks from each batch of cutoffs. The hardest part was trying to decide which bonus block to make from the cutoffs.

Double Pinwheels, 37¼" x 37¼", made by Nancy Johnson-Srebro and quilted by Veronica Nurmi.

These lively pinwheels make a perfect border for this wall-hanging. There are small pinwheels within the larger pinwheels. The quilting design adds even more movement to this quilt. These bonus cutoffs came from the 18" Block 22 used in Quilt Map 8 (page 116).

Bonus cutoffs from the 12" Block 28 for Quilt Map 3 (page 96) were used to create a stunning original block. The apparent movement was created because of the mirror images of the cutoffs. Notice the top left and bottom right are identical and the top right and bottom left are identical but opposites of each other. This would make a nice table topper to go with the table runner.

Whirligig, 25³/₄" x 25³/₄", *made by Nancy Johnson-Srebro and quilted by Veronica Nurmi.*

I really had fun designing this wallhanging with bonus cutoffs from eight 18" stars, (Block 22, used in Quilt Map 8 on page 116). There were so many ways I could position these pieces that I had a hard time deciding. The quilting design really enhances the beauty of this quilt. The pink-striped fabric was added to make this puzzle complete!

Puzzle Pieces, 47" x 47", *made by Nancy Johnson-Srebro and quilted by Veronica Nurmi.*

The lattice units from Quilt Map 2 (page 92) provided a wealth of flying geese for this darling miniature. The hint of autumn color comes from the cutoffs of the 8" Block 1 used in that quilt.

A Hint of Autumn, 22¹/₄" x 22¹/₄", *made by Nancy Johnson-Srebro and quilted by Veronica Nurmi.*

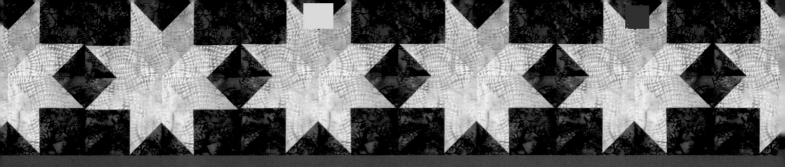

THINKING *INSIDE* THE BLOCK

I have to confess that I became so excited about this new method for making eight-pointed stars that I designed more star blocks than could be included in this book! *Stars by Magic* is just the beginning of what can be done with my Diamond-Free method. "Thinking Inside the Block" became my theme. It's easy to design when you don't look at a star as a whole block, but rather as four quarter-blocks.

As you can see, there are many ways to make Block 1 look different by simply changing the placement of color. But what would happen if just a quarter of Block 1 were used?

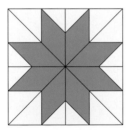

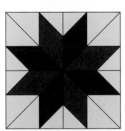
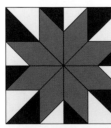

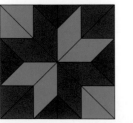
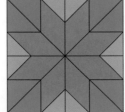

Quarter Blocks

Frame each quarter section with lattice strips and a cornerstone.

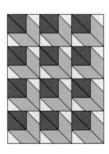

For an optical illusion, repeat the quarter section.

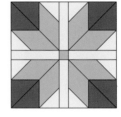

Make a stunning border from a quarter-block.

If a wider border is needed, rotate the quarter-block and add a second row.

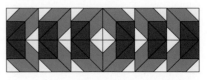

A lovely zigzag border appears when you position the quarter-blocks as shown below. Rectangles now frame the four large stars.

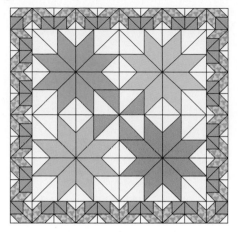

If you turn the quarter-blocks in the opposite direction, a half-star now surrounds the four large stars.

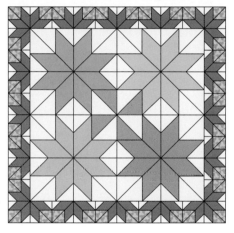

Half Blocks

Here are more examples using half-blocks for borders.

An interesting pattern is formed along the outer edges of this border.

Block 3

A large dark triangle appears to separate the half stars. This is accomplished by using two different fabrics for the corners of each block.

Block 15

A very striking border is formed from half-Lone Stars.

Block 9

Two rows of flying geese are created between these half-blocks.

Block 14

A definite zigzag is formed when placing these half-blocks together.

Block 28

This border looks as if it's exploding!

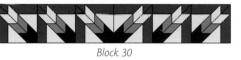

Block 30

One of my favorite ways to design a unique quilt is to take half-blocks and have them meet in the center. Keep in mind, all of this is done by cutting and sewing just squares and rectangles—the Diamond-Free way!

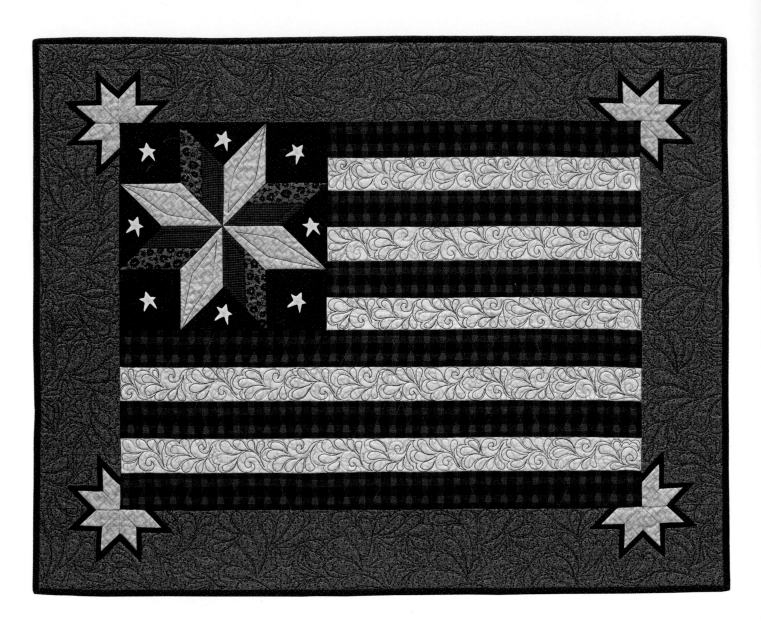

Quilt Map #1

QUILT SIZE: 32¹/₂" x 40¹/₂"
BLOCKS USED: 12" Block 11 (page 38)
6" Block 14 (page 44)

Flying High, made by Nancy Johnson-Srebro. Quilted by Sharon Schamber.

You can easily sew this fun patriotic quilt in just one day. The partial corner stars add a special feature to this quilted tribute to the American flag.

BLOCK 11
12" x 12"

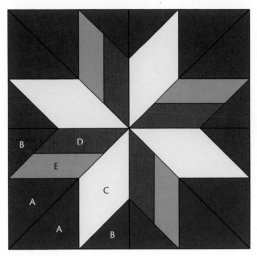

YARDAGE FOR ONE BLOCK

ITEM	COLOR	QUANTITY NEEDED
A, B	⬛	⅜ yard
C	⬜	8" x 14" strip
D	⬛	8" x 12" strip
E	⬛	8" x 12" strip

CUTTING FOR ONE BLOCK

ITEM	COLOR	# TO CUT	SIZE
A	⬛	8	4" x 6½"
B	⬛	8	3" x 3"
C	⬜	4	3" x 6½"
D	⬛	4	1¾" x 6½"
E	⬛	4	1¾" x 6½"

For sewing instructions, see page 39.
Note that values for A and B pieces are dark in this wallhanging.

YARDAGE FOR FOUR HALF AND FOUR QUARTER BLOCKS

ITEM	COLOR	QUANTITY NEEDED
A, B	⬛	⅜ yard
C	⬜	¼ yard
D, E	⬛	¼ yard

BLOCK 14
6" x 6"

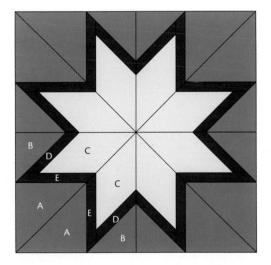

CUTTING FOR FOUR HALF AND FOUR QUARTER BLOCKS

ITEM	COLOR	# TO CUT	SIZE
A	⬛	24	2¼" x 3½"
B	⬛	24	1¾" x 1¾"
C	⬜	24	1½" x 2⅞"
D	⬛	24	1½" x 2⅛"
E	⬛	24	¾" x 3½"

For sewing instructions, see page 45.
Make four half-blocks and four quarter-blocks.
Note that values for A and B pieces are dark and C pieces are light in this wallhanging.

YARDAGE

ITEM	COLOR	QUANTITY NEEDED
A, B	■	½ yard
C, D	▫	⅜ yard
E, F, *G, *H	▪	¾ yard
*Binding	■	½ yard
Backing		39" x 47"

Based on cutting crosswise grain of the fabric.

CUTTING

ITEM	COLOR	# TO CUT	SIZE
A	■	3	2½" x 18½"
B	■	3	2½" x 30½"
C	▫	3	2½" x 18½"
D	▫	2	2½" x 30½"
E	▪	8	2½" x 3½"
F	▪	4	2½" x 8½"
G	▪	2	5½" x 16½"
H	▪	2	5½" x 24½"

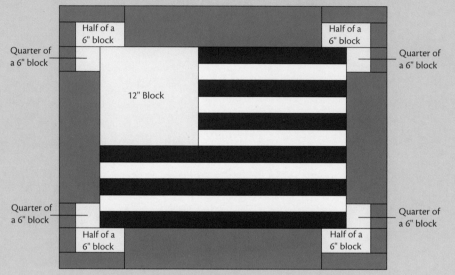

Quilt Diagram

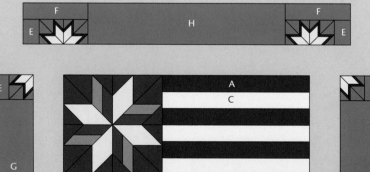

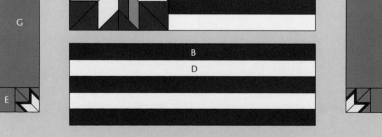

Piecing Diagram

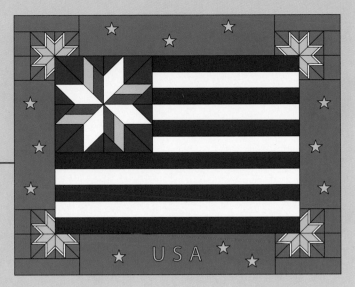

Option 1 *Use decorative threads to hand or machine embroider U.S.A. and small five-pointed stars in the border.*

Option 2 *For a contemporary look, add another 12" star and use a very dark background for the border and around the stars. Block 1 was used in the corners.*

Option 3 *For a totally different look, use four 6" stars in place of one 12" star. Again, the simpler Block 1 is shown at the corners.*

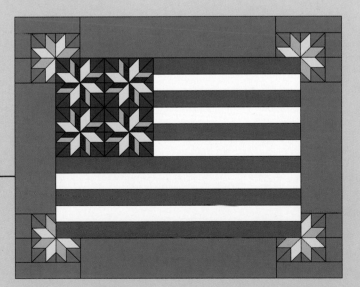

Quilt Map #2

QUILT SIZE: 49$^{1}/_{2}$" x 51$^{1}/_{2}$"
BLOCKS USED: 8" **Block 1** (page 18)

Batik Madness, made by Nancy Johnson-Srebro. Quilted by Sharon Schamber.

The stars and zigzag lattice strips really stand out against the dark background fabric. This is a wonderful quilt map to showcase some of your favorite fabrics, as I did here with batiks.

BLOCK 1
8" x 8"

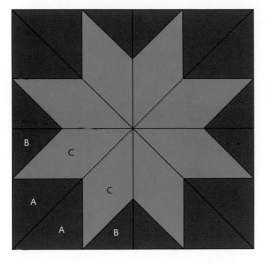

YARDAGE FOR FIFTEEN BLOCKS

ITEM	COLOR	QUANTITY NEEDED
A, B	■	1⅞ yards
C	■	6" x 22" strip of 15 different fabrics

CUTTING FOR FIFTEEN BLOCKS

ITEM	COLOR	# TO CUT	SIZE
A	■	120	2⅞" x 4½"
B	■	120	2⅛" x 2⅛"
*C	■	8	2⅛" x 4½"

Cut from each of the fifteen fabrics.
For sewing instructions, see page 19.
Note that values for A and B pieces are dark and C is medium in this quilt.

YARDAGE

ITEM	COLOR	QUANTITY NEEDED
*A	■	⅞ yard
B, *C, **D, **E, **F, *Binding	■	2½ yards
Backing		56" x 58"

Based on cutting crosswise grain of the fabric.
**Based on cutting lengthwise grain of the fabric.*

CUTTING

ITEM	COLOR	# TO CUT	SIZE
A	■	88	2½" x 4½"
B	■	176	2½" x 2½"
C	■	12	1½" x 8½"
*D	■	6	1½" x 44½"
*E	■	2	2" x 44½"
*F	■	2	4" x 49½"

Cut on the lengthwise grain before cutting B and C.

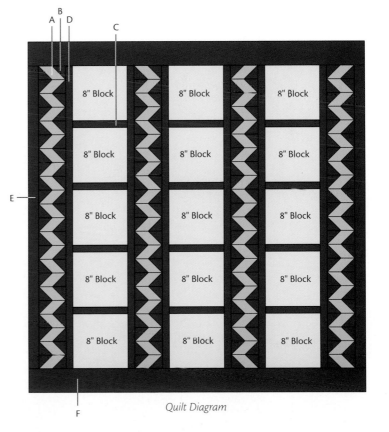

Quilt Diagram

Piecing Diagram

Sewing Instructions

Lattice Unit 1

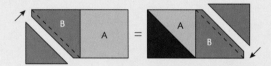

Make 44.
Use 11 in each vertical row.

Lattice Unit 2

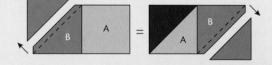

Make 44.
Use 11 in each vertical row

Option 1

This pared-down version of the original quilt map would make a jazzy table runner.

Option 2 *Make just a few more blocks for coordinating placemats.*

Option 3 *You will create a dynamic, yet totally different, quilt by simply rotating the original version. Use the same block throughout or use a different block in each row.*

Quilt Map #3

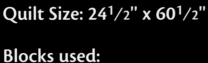

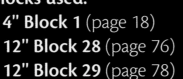

Quilt Size: 24¹/₂" x 60¹/₂"

Blocks used:
  4" Block 1 (page 18)
  12" Block 28 (page 76)
  12" Block 29 (page 78)

Star Harmony, made by Nancy Johnson-Srebro. Quilted by Veronica Nurmi.

The little stars add a touch of elegance to this table runner. The dark background allows each block to say, "Hey! Look at me!"

BLOCK 28
12" x 12"

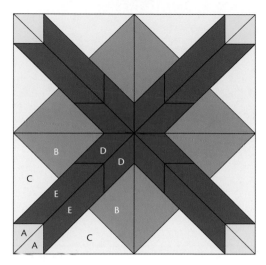

YARDAGE FOR TWO BLOCKS

ITEM	COLOR	QUANTITY NEEDED
A		¼ yard
B		½ yard
C		½ yard
D		¼ yard
E		½ yard

CUTTING FOR TWO BLOCKS

ITEM	COLOR	# TO CUT	SIZE
A		16	2" x 6½"
B		16	5" x 5"
C		16	5" x 5"
D		16	2" x 6½"
E		16	3½" x 6½"

For sewing instructions, see page 77.
Note that values for A pieces are light and D pieces are dark in this table runner.

YARDAGE FOR ONE BLOCK

ITEM	COLOR	QUANTITY NEEDED
A, C		¼ yard
B		⅜ yard
D		¼ yard
E		¼ yard

CUTTING FOR ONE BLOCK

ITEM	COLOR	# TO CUT	SIZE
A		8	2" x 6½"
B		8	5" x 5"
C		8	2" x 6½"
D		8	2" x 6½"
E		8	2" x 6½"

For sewing instructions, see page 79.
Note that values for A and B pieces are dark in this table runner.

BLOCK 29
12" x 12"

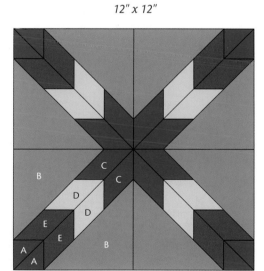

BLOCK 1
4" x 4"

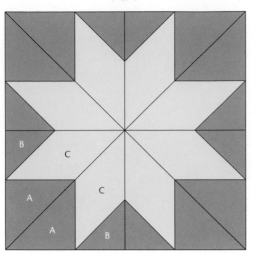

YARDAGE FOR SIX BLOCKS

ITEM	COLOR	QUANTITY NEEDED
A, B		⅜ yard
C		¼ yard

CUTTING FOR SIX BLOCKS

ITEM	COLOR	# TO CUT	SIZE
A		48	1⅝" x 2½"
B		48	1⅜" x 1⅜"
C		48	1⅜" x 2½"

For sewing instructions, see page 19.
Note that values for A and B pieces are dark and C pieces are light in this table runner.

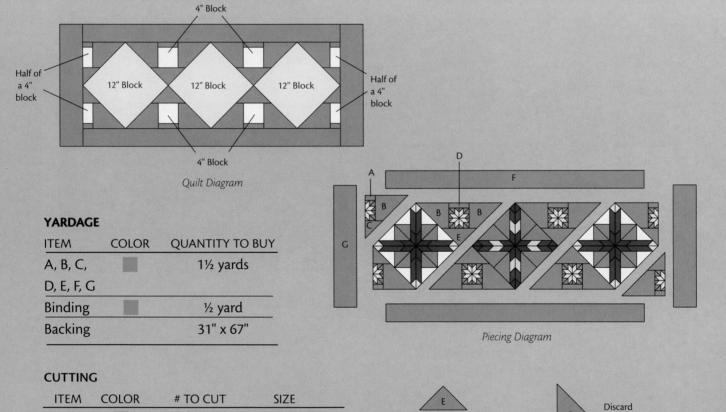

Quilt Diagram

YARDAGE

ITEM	COLOR	QUANTITY TO BUY
A, B, C, D, E, F, G		1½ yards
Binding		½ yard
Backing		31" x 67"

Piecing Diagram

CUTTING

ITEM	COLOR	# TO CUT	SIZE	
A		4	1½" x 2½"	
B		6	7⅜" x 7⅜"	◻
C		2	4⅜" x 4⅜"	◻
D		4	1½" x 4½"	
E		1	8¼" x 8¼"	⊠
*F		4	4" x 26"	
*G		2	5" x 24½"	

Based on cutting crosswise grain of the fabric. Piece two F strips together for the required length.

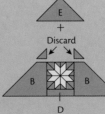

Make 4.
Trim B even with the star.

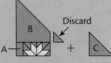

Make 2.
Trim B even with the star.

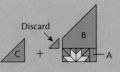

Make 2.
Trim B even with the star.

Option 1 *Make place mats to go with the table runner.*

Option 2 *Sew three table runners together vertically for a large wallhanging. Use dark fabrics around the 4" star blocks and for the border. Block 13 is featured as the large star block.*

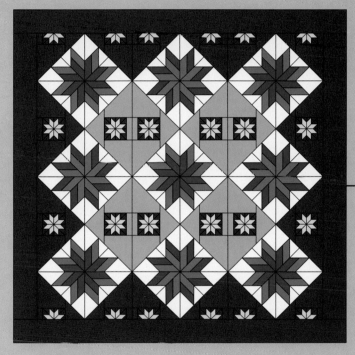

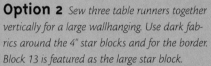

Option 3 *Achieve a totally different look when you piece three table runners together horizontally with lattice strips between each.*

Quilt Map #4

Quilt Size: 44³/4" x 44³/4"
Blocks used: 6" Block 23 (page 64)

Peony Passion, made by Nancy Johnson-Srebro. Quilted by Sharon Schamber.

Batik fabrics for the flowers and black for the background give this wall-hanging a contemporary Amish look. You may not notice at first glance, but the setting features the super-simple Churn Dash block. This quilt may look complex, but it's really quite easy.

BLOCK 23

6" x 6"

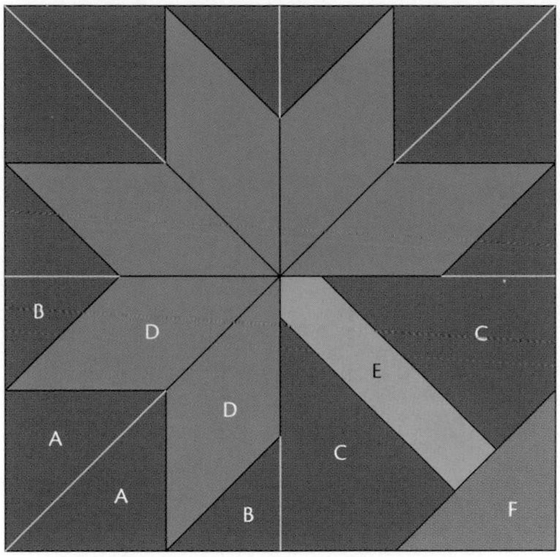

YARDAGE FOR NINE BLOCKS

ITEM	COLOR	QUANTITY NEEDED
A, B, C		⅞ yard
D		9" x 18" strip of 5 different fabrics
E		5" x 8" strip of 5 different fabrics
F		3" x 5" strip of 5 different fabrics

CUTTING FOR NINE BLOCKS

ITEM	COLOR	# TO CUT	SIZE
A		54	2¼" x 3½"
B		54	1¾" x 1¾"
C		18	3⅛" x 3⅛"
*D		12	1¾" x 3½"
*E		2	3½" x 3½"
*F		2	2⅛" x 2⅛"

**Cut from each of the five fabrics. There will be extra D, E, and F pieces.*

For sewing instructions, see page 65.

Note that values for A, B, C pieces are dark and D is medium in this wallhanging.

YARDAGE FOR FIVE BLOCKS

ITEM	COLOR	QUANTITY NEEDED
*A, *B		¼ yard of 5 different fabrics
C		⅛ yard of 5 different fabrics
*D		¼ yard

**These fabrics are also used in the quilt map. See page 102.*

CUTTING FOR FIVE BLOCKS

ITEM	COLOR	# TO CUT	Size
*A		2	3⅞" x 3⅞"
*B		1	2" x 30"
*C		1	2" x 30"
D		10	3⅞" x 3⅞"

**Cut from each of the five fabrics.*

CHURN DASH BLOCK

12" x 12"

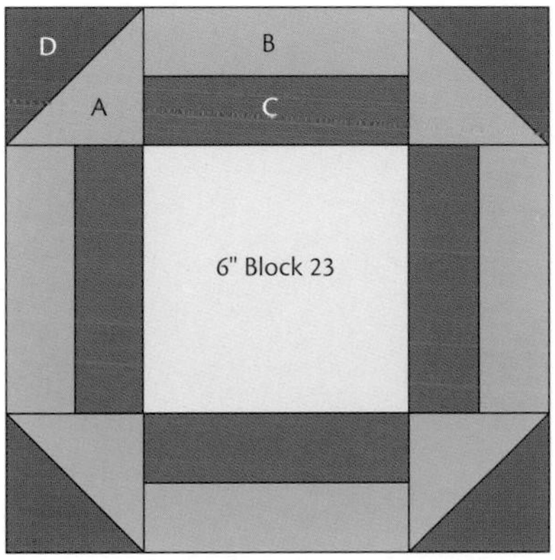

Sewing Instructions

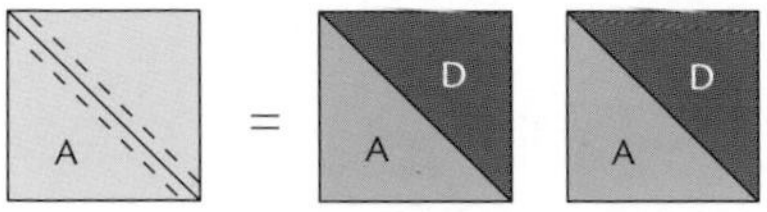

Place A on top of D, stitch, and cut to produce two triangle squares (see page 9). You need a total of four A/D squares per block.

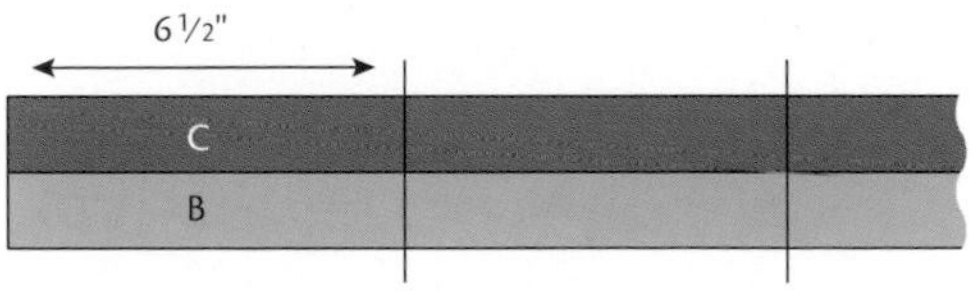

Sew B to C. Cut into 4 segments 6 1/2" each.

ITEM	COLOR	QUANTITY NEEDED
A, B		Use A/B fabrics left from the Churn Dash blocks.
C, D, E, F, G, H, I, Binding		1¾ yards
Backing		51" x 51"

CUTTING

ITEM	COLOR	# TO CUT	SIZE
*A		1	3½" x 3½"
**B		2	2⅝" x 4¾"
C		4	2⅝" x 17½"
D		4	2⅝" x 9"
E		4	2⅝" x 11⅛"
F		2	9⅜" x 9⅜" ◹
G		2	9¾" x 9¾" ⊠
H		2	3½" x 38¾"
***I		4	3½" x 22⅝"

*Cut one from each of the A/B Churn Dash fabrics used in the four outer blocks.

**Cut two from each of the A/B Churn Dash fabrics used in the four outer blocks.

***Piece two border strips together for the required length.

Piecing Borders

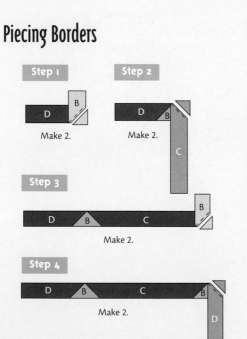

Step 1
Make 2.

Step 2
Make 2.

Step 3
Make 2.

Step 4
Make 2.

Repeat Steps 1–4 for the top and bottom borders using B, C, and E pieces.

Note: Be sure to use the correct color B rectangles when piecing the borders.

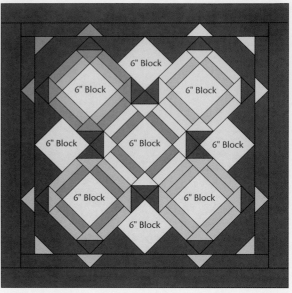

Quilt Diagram

Piecing Diagram

Option 1 *Simplify the quilt by piecing fewer blocks. Look what happens when you replace the four outer blocks with solid squares.*

Option 2 *Set the Churn Dash blocks together with a Four-Patch block consisting of two pieced blocks and two solid blocks. Wouldn't this look great in plaids and stripes?*

Option 3 *Set the Churn Dash blocks side by side to create a secondary block pattern.*

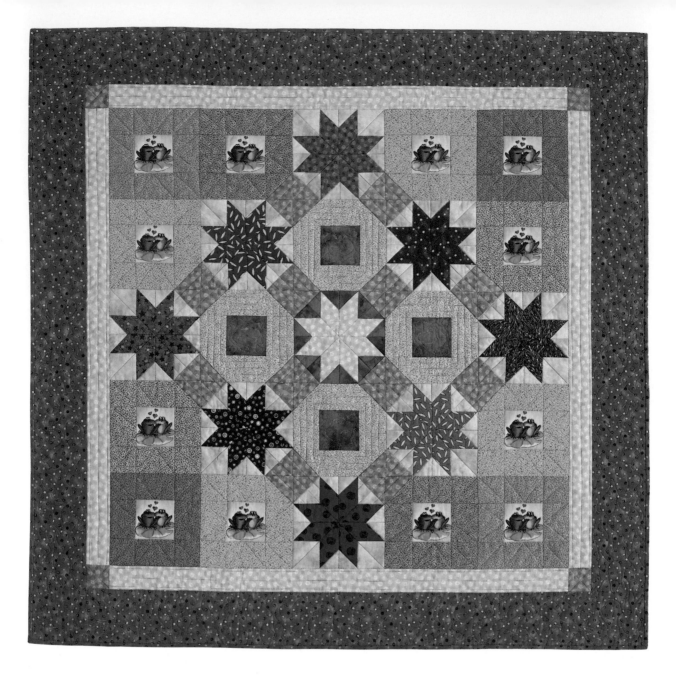

Quilt Map #5

Quilt Size: 53¹/2" x 53¹/2"
Blocks used: 8" Block 2 (page 20)

Star Parade, made by Nancy Johnson-Srebro. Quilted by Veronica Nurmi.

Look what two of the easiest quilt blocks can make! Color placement is the fun part of this baby quilt.

BLOCK 2
8" x 8"

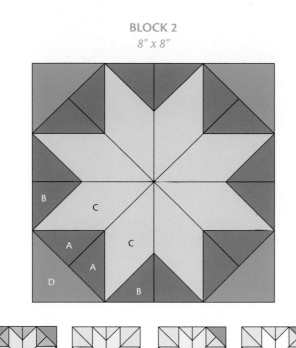

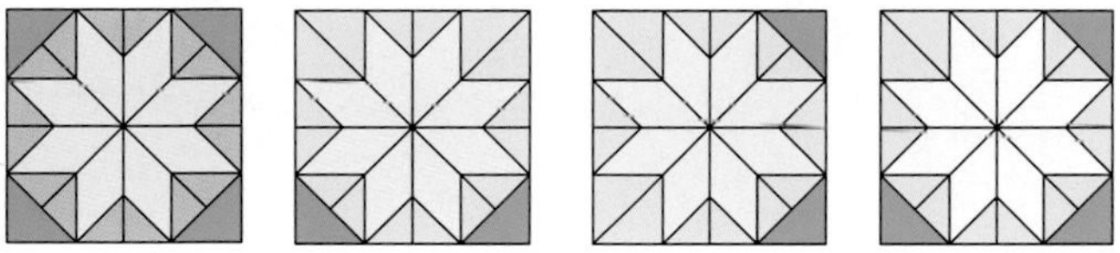

| Make 1. | Make 2. | Make 2. | Make 4. |

YARDAGE FOR NINE BLOCKS

ITEM	COLOR	QUANTITY NEEDED
A, B		1 yard for 8 stars
		¼ yard for center star
C		6" x 22" strip of 9
		different fabrics
D		¼ yard

CUTTING FOR NINE BLOCKS

ITEM	COLOR	# TO CUT	SIZE
A		64 for eight stars	2⅞" x 4½"
		8 for center star	
B		64 for eight stars	2⅛" x 2⅛"
		8 for center star	
*C		8	2⅛" x 4½"
D		24	2⅞" x 2⅞"

Cut from each of the nine fabrics.
For sewing instructions, see page 21.
Note that values for A and B pieces are dark for the center star. See the block diagrams at left for placement of D and the Piecing Diagram on page 106 for placement of each block.

SQUARE-WITHIN-A-SQUARE
8" x 8"

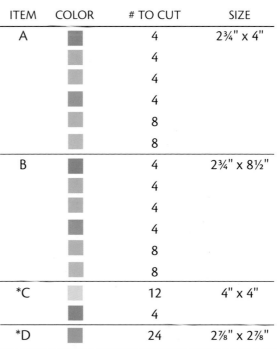

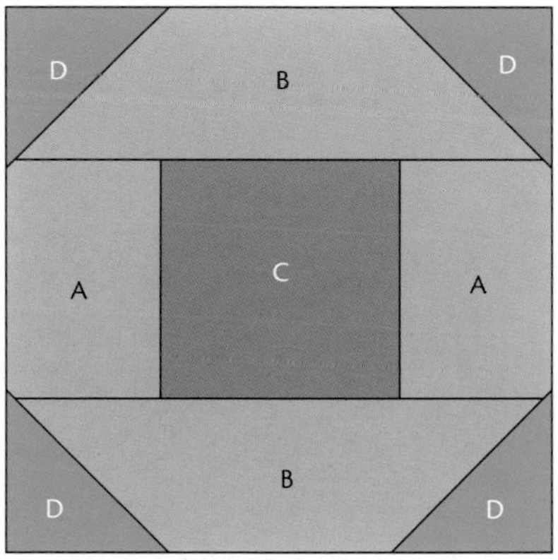

YARDAGE FOR SIXTEEN BLOCKS

ITEM	COLOR	QUANTITY NEEDED
A, B		¼ yard each of 4 different fabrics
		(Each color will make 2 blocks.)
		⅜ yard each of 2 different fabrics
		(Each color will make 4 blocks.)
*C		⅜ yard for 12 blocks
		¼ yard for 4 blocks
D		¼ yard

Buy more fabric if fussy cutting these pieces.

CUTTING FOR SIXTEEN BLOCKS

ITEM	COLOR	# TO CUT	SIZE
A		4	2¾" x 4"
		4	
		4	
		4	
		8	
		8	
B		4	2¾" x 8½"
		4	
		4	
		4	
		8	
		8	
*C		12	4" x 4"
		4	
*D		24	2⅞" x 2⅞"

See the sewing instructions on page 106 for placement of C and D in each block.

Sewing Instructions

Refer to the *Piecing Diagram* below for placement of each block. If you fussy cut your fabric for C, be sure to rotate each block to its correct orientation before adding the D squares on the corners, so the center fabric squares will be going the right direction.

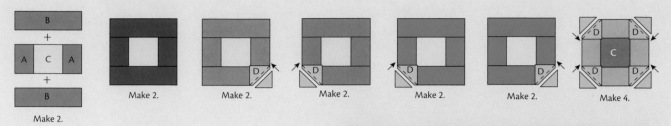

Make 2.	Make 2.	Make 2.	Make 2.	Make 2.	Make 2.	Make 4.

YARDAGE

ITEM	COLOR	QUANTITY NEEDED
*A		⅝ yard
**B		⅛ yard
*C, *D		1¼ yards
*Binding		½ yard
Backing		60" x 60"

*Based on cutting crosswise grain of the fabric.

**Or use scraps from block fabric D.

CUTTING

ITEM	COLOR	# TO CUT	SIZE
*A		8	2½" x 20½"
B		4	2½" x 2½"
*C		4	5" x 22½"
*D		4	5" x 27"

*Piece two border strips together for the required length.

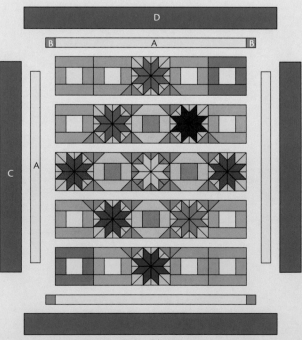

Quilt Diagram

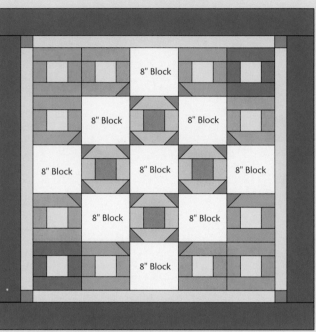

Piecing Diagram

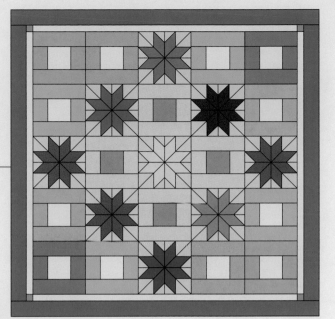

Option 1 *Making a quilt is a step-by-step process. Don't be afraid to change your mind during this time. I call this "Thinking Inside the Block." The following diagrams show you how I used this concept. The quilt started out with Block 1 and a simple Square-Within-a-Square block set side by side.*

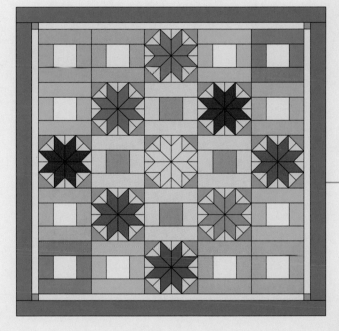

Option 2 *I used Block 2 in this option. It made the quilt a little more interesting to the eye.*

Option 3 *For the final design, I decided to see what would happen if I modified Block 2 and the Square-Within-a-Square by placing a contrasting fabric on some of the adjoining corners. The center star with contrasting fabric on all four corners is the only "true" Block 2 in this quilt! See how easy it is to think inside the block?*

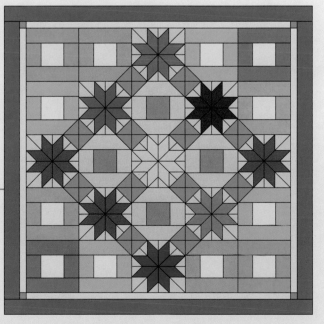

Quilt Map #6

Quilt Size: 49" x 49"
Blocks used: 10" Block 14 (page 44)
              10" Block 27 (page 74)

Celestial Seasons, made by Janet McCarroll. Quilted by Veronica Nurmi.

Luscious hand-dyed fabrics make this quilt glow! An exciting, secondary diagonal design emerges when Block 27 is used as an alternate block and cornerstones are added to the lattice strips. For extra pizzazz, Janet added cornerstones on the four corners and in the inner border of the quilt.

BLOCK 14
10" x 10"

YARDAGE FOR FIVE BLOCKS

ITEM	COLOR	QUANTITY NEEDED
A, B		1 yard
C		6" x 22" strip of 5 different fabrics
D, E		¼ yard of 5 different fabrics

CUTTING FOR FIVE BLOCKS

ITEM	COLOR	# TO CUT	SIZE
A		40	3½" x 5½"
B		40	2½" x 2½"
*C		8	2⅛" x 4⅝"
*D		8	2⅛" x 3"
*E		8	⅞" x 5½"

Cut from each of the five fabrics.
For sewing instructions, see page 45.

BLOCK 27
10" x 10"

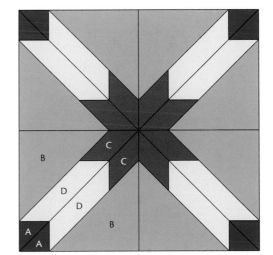

YARDAGE FOR FOUR BLOCKS

ITEM	COLOR	QUANTITY NEEDED
A		⅜ yard
B		⅝ yard
C		7" x 22" strip of 4 different fabrics
D		⅝ yard

CUTTING FOR FOUR BLOCKS

ITEM	COLOR	# TO CUT	SIZE
A		32	1¾" x 5½"
B		32	4¼" x 4¼"
*C		8	1¾" x 5½"
D		32	3" x 5½"

* *Cut from each of the four fabrics.*
For sewing instructions, see page 75.

YARDAGE

ITEM	COLOR	QUANTITY NEEDED
A		¼ yard
*B		½ yard
C, *D, *E		⅜ yard
*F, *G		1¼ yard
*Binding		½ yard
Backing		55" x 55"

*Based on cutting crosswise grain of the fabric.

CUTTING

ITEM	COLOR	# TO CUT	SIZE
A		36	1¾" x 1¾"
B		24	1¾" x 10½"
C		8	1¾" x 1¾"
D		8	1¾" x 8"
E		4	1¾" x 13"
F		2	6" x 38"
*G		4	6" x 24¾"

*Piece two border strips together for the required length.

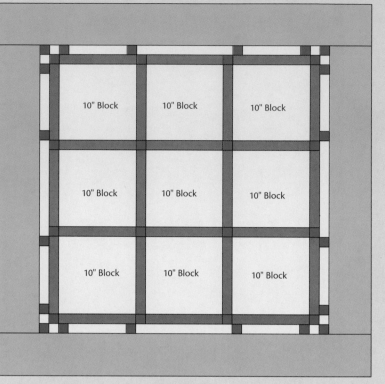

Quilt Diagram

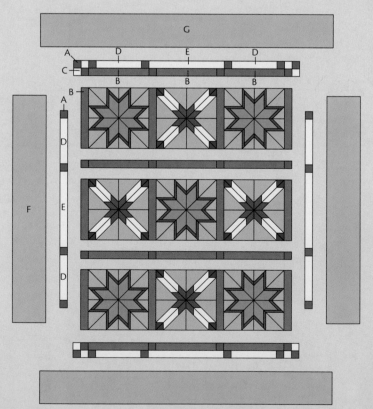

Piecing Diagram

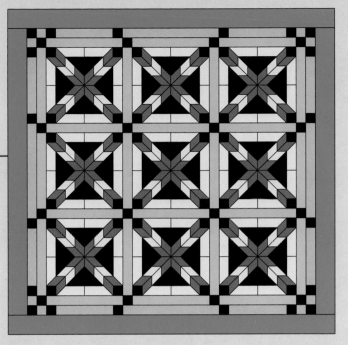

Option 1 *There's nothing boring about this straight set if you use Block 30!*

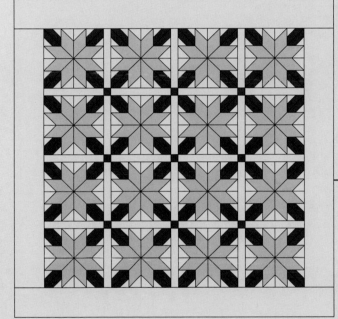

Option 2 *A straight set works really well with many of the blocks in this book. A secondary design is formed when you use Block 6.*

Option 3 *Stars and more stars are formed when you use the straight set with Block 21.*

Quilt Map #7

Quilt Size: 41" x 41"
Blocks used: 6" and 10" Block 20 (page 56)

Snow Crystals, made by Nancy Johnson-Srebro. Quilted by Sharon Schamber.

You can't go wrong with a classic blue-and-white wallhanging. Using a white-on-white fabric for part of the blocks emphasizes their snowflake look, and the half-blocks in the border make this wallhanging sparkle!

BLOCK 20
6" x 6"

YARDAGE FOR FOUR BLOCKS

ITEM	COLOR	QUANTITY NEEDED
A, B, C	■	⅜ yard
D	□	¼ yard
E, F	■	¼ yard

CUTTING FOR FOUR BLOCKS

ITEM	COLOR	# TO CUT	SIZE
A	■	32	2¼" x 3½"
B	■	32	1⅛" x 2"
C	■	32	1⅛" x 1⅛"
D	□	32	1⅛" x 2⅞"
E	■	32	1⅛" x 1¾"
F	■	32	1⅛" x 2⅝"

For sewing instructions, see page 57.
Note that values for A, B, and C pieces are dark and D pieces are light in this wallhanging.

YARDAGE FOR EIGHT HALF-BLOCKS

ITEM	COLOR	QUANTITY NEEDED
A, B, C	■	1 yard
D	□	⅜ yard
E, F	■	⅜ yard

CUTTING FOR EIGHT HALF-BLOCKS

ITEM	COLOR	# TO CUT	SIZE
A	■	32	3½" x 5½"
B	■	32	1½" x 3"
C	■	32	1½" x 1½"
D	□	32	1½" x 4½"
E	■	32	1½" x 2½"
F	■	32	1½" x 4"

For sewing instructions, see page 57.
Make eight half-blocks.
Note that values for A, B, and C pieces are dark and D pieces are light in this wallhanging.

BLOCK 20 (half)
5" x 10"

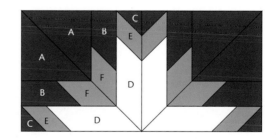

YARDAGE

ITEM	COLOR	QUANTITY NEEDED
A, B, C, D, E		⅝ yard
F, G, H, I, J, K		1⅛ yards
Binding		½ yard
Backing		47" x 47"

CUTTING

ITEM	COLOR	# TO CUT	SIZE
A		4	3½" x 3½"
B		8	3⅞" x 3⅞"
C		4	2" x 9½"
D		2	3" x 20"
E		2	3" x 25"
F		8	3⅞" x 3⅞"
G		1	2" x 2"
H		8	2" x 5½"
I		4	5½" x 7"
J		2	3½" x 35"
*K		4	3½" x 20¾"

*Piece two border strips together for the required length.

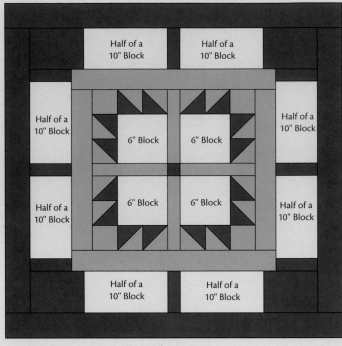

Quilt Diagram

Place B on top of F and stitch to produce two squares. You need a total of sixteen B/F squares.

Piecing Diagram

Option 1 *A super-simple wallhanging could be made with just four 6" blocks.*

Option 2 *Create a stunning wallhanging with half-blocks. The half-blocks meet in the middle to create a full block.*

Option 3 *Use the center of this quilt map to showcase a special appliqué block. The finished size of the center square for the appliqué background is 19$\frac{1}{2}$".*

Quilt Map #8

Quilt Size: 87$^{1}/_{2}$" x 104"
Blocks used: 9" Block 1 (page 18)
               18" Block 22 (page 61)

Enlightenment, made by Nancy Johnson-Srebro. Quilted by Sharon Schamber.

One simple quilt map + two great blocks = one extraordinary quilt! Notice how the quilting design and thread enhance the quilt.

BLOCK 1
9" x 9"

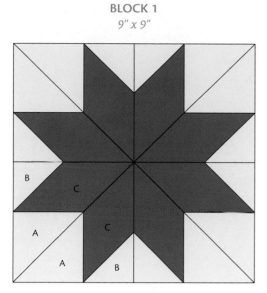

YARDAGE FOR SEVEN BLOCKS

ITEM	COLOR	QUANTITY NEEDED
A, B		1⅛ yards
C		7" x 22" strip of 7 different fabrics

CUTTING FOR SEVEN BLOCKS

ITEM	COLOR	# TO CUT	SIZE
A		56	3⅛" x 5"
B		56	2⅜" x 2⅜"
*C		8	2⅜" x 5"

*Cut from each of the seven fabrics.
For sewing instructions, see page 19.

YARDAGE FOR EIGHT BLOCKS

ITEM	COLOR	QUANTITY NEEDED
A, B, C		3½ yards
D		7" x 22" strip of 8 different fabrics
E		⅜ yard of 8 different fabrics
F, G		½ yard of 8 different fabrics

CUTTING FOR EIGHT BLOCKS

ITEM	COLOR	# TO CUT	SIZE
A		64	3⅞" x 9½"
B		64	4¼" x 4¼"
C		64	2⅜" x 3⅛"
*D		8	2⅜" x 5"
*E		16	2⅜" x 6⅞"
*F		8	2⅜" x 5"
*G		8	2⅜" x 8¾"

* Cut from each of the eight fabrics.
For sewing instructions, see page 62.

BLOCK 22
18" x 18"

YARDAGE

ITEM	COLOR	QUANTITY NEEDED
A, *B, *C, *D, *E, *F		3⅝ yards
*G, *H		½ yard
**I, **J		2⅝ yards
K		⅜ yard
*Binding		1 yard
Backing		94" x 110"

*Based on cutting crosswise grain of the fabric.
**Based on cutting lengthwise grain of the fabric.

CUTTING

ITEM	COLOR	# TO CUT	SIZE
A		14	7¼" x 7¼"
B		8	7⅝" x 13¼"
C		6	3⅛" x 13¼"
D		2	7⅝" x 18½"
E		12	5" x 18½"
F		4	5" x 27½"
G		5	1½" x 40"
H		4	1½" x 40"
*I		2	8" x 89"
*J		2	8" x 72½"
K		4	8" x 8"

*If you are using a stripe fabric for the borders, cut nine 8" strips on the crosswise grain. Sew the strips together and cut to the correct length.

Flat Piping Instructions

G and H strips create a flat piping that finishes at ½" wide. Sew the short ends of the strips together. Press the strips in half lengthwise with wrong sides together so they measure ¾" wide. Trim these strips to the length/width of the quilt and follow the sewing diagrams below.

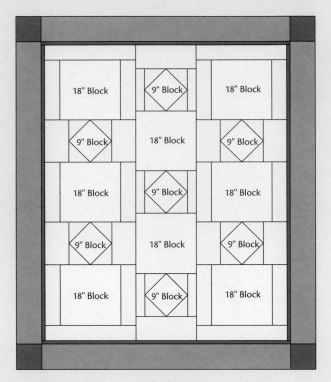

Quilt Diagram

Piecing Diagram

Align the raw edges of the piping with the top/bottom of the quilt. Stitch as before.

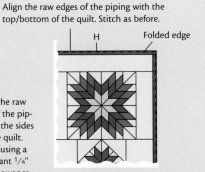

Folded edge

Folded edge

G

H

Align the raw edges of the piping with the sides of the quilt. Stitch, using a very scant ¼" seam allowance.

Make 7.

Option 1 *For a smaller wallhanging, eliminate four of the 18" blocks and two 9" blocks. To make the star blocks stand out, use a darker fabric for the lattice strips.*

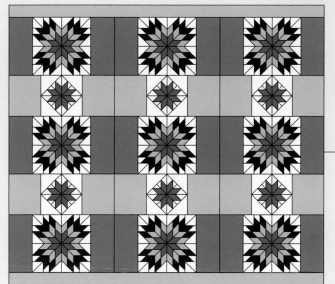

Option 2 *Replace the center row with a repeat of the outer rows for an exciting and very different look. Use two different fabrics for the lattice strips to create horizontal and vertical interest.*

Option 3 *Your guests will be truly impressed by this table runner. It features the middle vertical row from the quilt map. Add side borders and prepare for rave reviews!*

Quilt Map #9

Quilt Size: 78¹/₂" x 90¹/₂"
Blocks used: All blocks are 10"

Block 2 (page 20)	**Block 8** (page 32)	**Block 15** (page 46)	**Block 20** (page 56)
Block 3 (page 22)	**Block 9** (page 34)	**Block 16** (page 48)	**Block 21** (page 58)
Block 5 (page 26)	**Block 12** (page 40)	**Block 17** (page 50)	**Block 22** (page 61)
Block 6 (page 28)	**Block 13** (page 42)	**Block 18** (page 52)	
Block 7 (page 30)	**Block 14** (page 44)	**Block 19** (page 54)	

Morning Star, made and quilted by Sharon Schamber.

Sometimes a simple quilt map is all that's needed to showcase lots of stunning blocks. This updated version of a sampler quilt allows each star to twist, turn, and sparkle. The quilting design really enhances the beauty of this quilt. Sharon chose 18 different blocks for her sampler quilt. Mix and match blocks to your heart's content to create your own unique quilt.

YARDAGE

ITEM	COLOR	QUANTITY NEEDED
A, B, *C, *D		4⅝ yards
Background for 18 Star blocks		3 yards
18 Star blocks		Various scraps**
*Binding		⅞ yard
Backing		85" x 97"

*Based on cutting crosswise grain of the fabric.
**Or see individual star blocks for cutting instructions to estimate yardages.

CUTTING

ITEM	COLOR	# TO CUT	SIZE
A		1	38½" x 50½"
B		18	2½" x 10½"
*C		4	10½" x 35½"
*D		4	10½" x 39½"

NOTE: See individual star blocks for cutting and sewing instructions.
*Piece two border strips together for the required length.

Quilt Diagram

Block 2	Block 12	Block 18	Block 5	Block 6
Block 14				Block 17
Block 22				Block 13
Block 19				Block 8
Block 20				Block 16
Block 3	Block 9	Block 15	Block 7	Block 21

Quilt Diagram

Quilting design, copyright Sharon Schamber

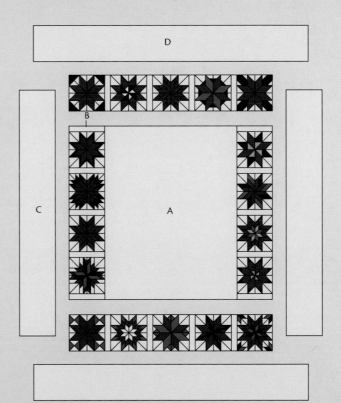

Piecing Diagram

Sharon is a master of feathered quilting designs, and this quilt map is the perfect backdrop for her talents. The feathers in both the center and border are also trapuntoed. The scrollwork designs in the center are echoed in the corners, and a simplified version was quilted between the blocks to tie the entire masterpiece together. Use this design as inspiration for your own quilt or create your own designs to fill the spaces. This is a wonderful opportunity for both machine and hand quilters to showcase their handiwork.

Quilt Map #10

Quilt Size: 62¹/₂" x 62¹/₂"
Blocks used: **6" Block 24** (page 66)
　　　　　　　8" Block 17 (page 50)
　　　　　　　18" Block 9 (page 34)

Medallion Chorus, made by Nancy Johnson-Srebro. Quilted by Veronica Nurmi.

The use of triple lattice strips, traditional blocks, and wonderful antique-looking fabrics makes this medallion quilt really stand out. For a smaller wallhanging, use only the center block and four small surrounding blocks.

BLOCK 9
18" x 18"

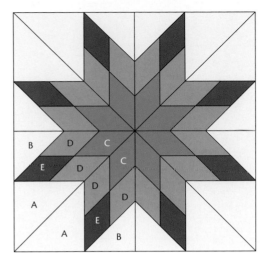

YARDAGE FOR ONE BLOCK

ITEM	COLOR	QUANTITY NEEDED
A, B		⅝ yard
C		¼ yard
D		⅜ yard
E		¼ yard

CUTTING FOR ONE BLOCK

ITEM	COLOR	# TO CUT	SIZE
A		8	5¾" x 9½"
B		8	4¼" x 4¼"
C		8	2⅜" x 5"
D		16	2⅜" x 6⅞"
E		8	2⅜" x 5"

For sewing instructions, see page 35.

YARDAGE FOR FOUR BLOCKS

ITEM	COLOR	QUANTITY NEEDED
A, B, C		⅜ yard
D		5" x 8" strip of 4 different fabrics
E, F		7" x 7" square of 4 different fabrics

CUTTING FOR FOUR BLOCKS

ITEM	COLOR	# TO CUT	SIZE
A		16	2¼" x 3½"
B		16	1¾" x 1¾"
C		8	3½" x 3½"
*D		4	1¾" x 3½"
*E		1	3½" x 6½"
*F		2	2⅜" x 2⅜"

Cut from each of the four fabrics.
For sewing instructions, see page 67.

BLOCK 24
6" x 6"

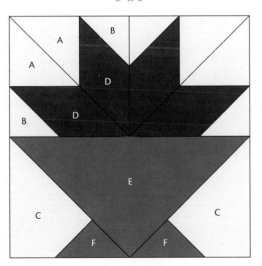

BLOCK 17
8" x 8"
Variation 1

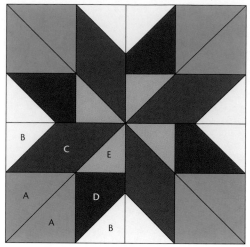

YARDAGE FOR FOUR BLOCKS

ITEM	COLOR	QUANTITY NEEDED
A		½ yard
B		¼ yard
C		6" x 10" strip of 4 different fabrics
D		4" x 13" strip of 4 different fabrics
E		⅛ yard

CUTTING FOR FOUR BLOCKS

ITEM	COLOR	# TO CUT	SIZE
A		32	2⅞" x 4½"
B		32	2⅛" x 2⅛"
*C		4	2⅛" x 4½"
*D		4	2⅛" x 2⅞"
E		16	2⅛" x 2⅛"

Cut from each of the four fabrics.
For sewing instructions, see page 51.

YARDAGE FOR FOUR BLOCKS

ITEM	COLOR	QUANTITY NEEDED
A, B		⅝ yard
C		6" x 10" strip of 4 different fabrics
D		4" x 13" strip of 4 different fabrics
E		⅛ yard

CUTTING FOR FOUR BLOCKS

ITEM	COLOR	# TO CUT	SIZE
A		32	2⅞" x 4½"
B		32	2⅛" x 2⅛"
*C		4	2⅛" x 4½"
*D		4	2⅛" x 2⅞"
E		16	2⅛" x 2⅛"

Cut from each of the four fabrics.
For sewing instructions, see page 51.

BLOCK 17
8" x 8"
Variation 2

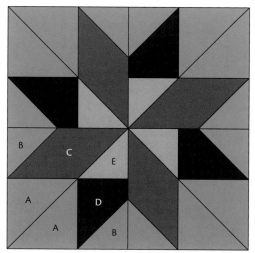

YARDAGE

ITEM	COLOR	QUANTITY TO BUY
A		¼ yard of 2 different fabrics
B		⅛ yard
*C, F		⅝ yard
D		3" x 10" strip
E		⅝ yard
G, H		2 yards
Binding		¾ yard
Backing		69" x 69

Based on cutting crosswise grain of the fabric.

CUTTING

ITEM	COLOR	# TO CUT	SIZE
*A		4	3" x 18½"
B		4	1½" x 18½"
C		4	2" x 30½"
D		4	2" x 2"
E		16	3⅜" x 13"
F		8	2¾" x 13"
**G		2	7" x 49½"
**H		2	7" x 62½"

Cut from each of the two fabrics.
**Based on cutting lengthwise grain of the fabric.*

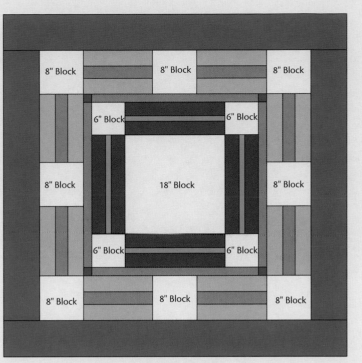

Quilt Diagram

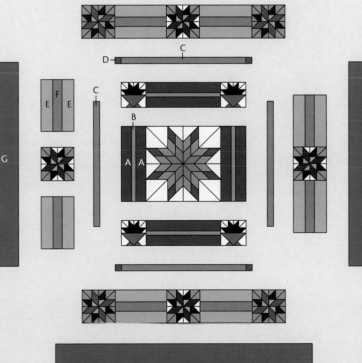

Piecing Diagram

Option 1 *This smaller, five-block version of the medallion wallhanging could easily be sewn in a day.*

Option 2 *Use triple lattice strips with any 8" block. Add solid vertical strips and embellish with appliqué.*

Option 3 *For an easy, but very striking, quilt combine an 8" block with the triple lattice strips. Start every other row with a star block and the opposite rows with the triple lattice strips.*

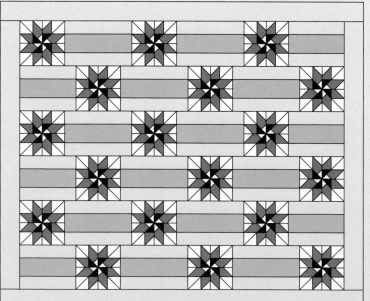

RESOURCES

American & Efird, Inc.
P.O. Box 507
Mt. Holly, NC 28120
www.amefird.com

Bernina® of America
3702 Prairie Lake Drive
Aurora, IL 60504
www.berninausa.com

Clearwater Fabrics
2 Bridge Street
Suite 220
Irvington, NY 10533
www.clearwaterfabrics.com

CLOTHWORKS
A division of Fabric Sales Co., Inc.
6250 Stanley Avenue South
Seattle, WA 98108
www.clothworks-fabric.com

Fairfield
www.poly-fil.com

FreeSpirit
1350 Broadway
21st Floor
New York, NY 10018
www.freespiritfabric.com

Just Another Button Company
116 West Market Street
Troy, IL 62294
(wholesale source)
www.justanotherbuttoncompany.com

Mountain Mist
2551 Crescentville Road
Cincinnati, OH 45241
www.stearnstextiles.com

P&B Textiles
1580 Gilbreth Road
Burlingame, CA 94010
www.pbtex.com

Prym Dritz Corporation/ Omnigrid®
P. O. Box 5028
Spartanburg, SC 29304
www.dritz.com

Quilting Creations International
PO Box 512
Zoar, OH 44697
www.quiltingcreations.com

Red Rooster Fabrics
1359 Broadway
Suite 1202
New York, NY 10018

RJR Fashion Fabrics
2203 Dominguez St.
Torrance, CA 90501
www.rjrfabrics.com

Robert Kaufman Co, Inc.
129 W. 132nd St.
Los Angeles, CA 90061
www.robertkaufman.com

Starr Designs
P.O. Box 440
Etna, CA 96027
www.starrfabrics.com

Superior Threads
P.O. Box 1672
St. George, UT 84771
www.superiorthreads.com

Timeless Treasures
483 Broadway
New York, NY 10013
www.ttfabrics.com

The Warm Company
954 E. Union St.
Seattle, WA 98122
www.warmcompany.com

About THE AUTHOR

Grandma Garrison was Nancy's mentor while she made her first quilt in 1972.

Nancy is highly sought after as a quilt-piecing designer, teacher, lecturer, and show judge. She refined how to work with squares and rectangles in her best selling books *Block Magic* and *Block Magic, Too!* Her leading-edge Quilt Map® concept allows the quilter to design his or her own quilts without any hassles. She has been a spokesperson for Omnigrid, a division of Prym Dritz, for over 13 years.

Nancy lives in eastern Pennsylvania with her husband, Frank. They have three grown children and one granddaughter. She travels extensively to teach and lecture on the wonderful art of quiltmaking. You can learn more about Nancy at www.nancyjohnsonsrebro.com.

Other fine books by Nancy Johnson-Srebro

Enter the Stars by Magic contest

Go to **www.ctpub.com**
Click on "For Quilters & Crafters"
under Services (left-hand bar)
for complete details!